Fodor's
25 Best

DUBAI

How to Use This Book

KEY TO SYMBOLS

✚ Map reference to the accompanying fold-out map

✉ Address

☎ Telephone number

🕑 Opening/closing times

🍴 Restaurant or café

🚆 Nearest rail station

Ⓜ Nearest subway (Metro) station

🚌 Nearest bus route

🛥 Nearest riverboat or ferry stop

♿ Facilities for visitors with disabilities

❓ Other practical information

▷ Further information

ℹ Tourist information

✋ Admission charges: Expensive (over 75 AED), Moderate (30–75 AED) and Inexpensive (30 AED or less)

This guide is divided into four sections

• **Essential Dubai:** An introduction to the city and tips on making the most of your stay.
• **Dubai by Area:** We've broken the city into five areas, and recommended the best sights, shops, entertainment venues, nightlife and restaurants in each one.
• **Where to Stay:** The best hotels, whether you're looking for luxury, budget or something in between.
• **Need to Know:** The info you need to make your trip run smoothly, including getting about by public transport, weather tips, emergency phone numbers and useful websites.

Navigation In the Dubai by Area chapter, we've given each area its own color, which is also used on the locator maps throughout the book and the map on the inside front cover.

Maps The fold-out map accompanying this book is a comprehensive street plan of Dubai. The grid on this fold-out map is the same as the grid on the locator maps within the book. We've given grid references within the book for each sight and listing.

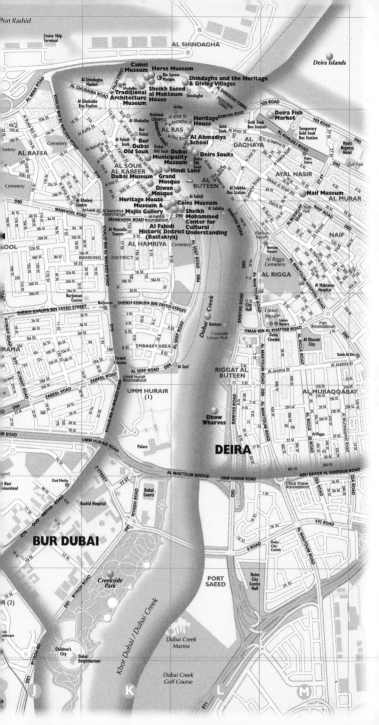

Port Rashid

Cruise Ship Terminal

AL SHINDAGHA

Deira Islands

Camel Museum
Horse Museum
Bin Suroor Mosque
Shindagha and the Heritage & Diving Villages
Al Shindagha Market
Traditional Architecture Museum
Sheikh Saeed al Maktoum House
Al Ghubaiba Bus Station
AL GHUBAIBA ROAD
Shindagha

Deira Fish Market
103 ROAD
Gold Souk Bus Station
Temporary Gold Souk Bus Station
Hyatt Regency Hotel
Golf Park

National Library
Heritage House
AL DAGHAYA
Palm Deira

Al Ghubaiba
Al Raffa
Bur Dubai Old Souk
Al Fahidi Souk
Bur Dubai Old Souk
AL RAS
Al Ahmadiya School
Deira Souks
AYAL NASIR

Dubai Municipality Museum
Hindi Lane
Deira Old Souk
AL BUTEEN
Naif Museum
AL MURAR

Grand Mosque
Diwan Mosque
Dubai Museum
AL SOUK AL KABEER
Al Sabkha Bus Station
NAIF

Heritage House Museum & Majlis Gallery
Coins Museum
Sheikh Mohammed Center for Cultural Understanding
Al Fahidi Historic District (Bastakiya)
AL HAMRIYA DISTRICT
AL SEEF ROAD
AL RIGGA
Al Rigga Cemetery
Baniyas Square

Dubai Creek
SHEIKH KHALIFA BIN ZAYED STREET
Burjuman Centre
Banking
Union Square
Fish Roundabout

Burjuman
EMBASSY AREA
Baniyas
Creekside Leisure Park
Deira Cinema
Al Ghurair City

Strand Cinema
AL SEEF ROAD
Al Seef
RIGGAT AL BUTEEN
AL MURAQQABAT

ZABEEL ROAD
Umm Hurair Roundabout
UMM HURAIR (I)
Palace

KHALID BIN AL WALEED ROAD
UMM HURAIR ROAD
Dhow Wharves
DEIRA

AL MAKTOUM BRIDGE
UMM HURAIR ROAD
ABU BAKER AL SIDDIQUE ROAD
Clock Tower Roundabout

Oud Metha
Nasr Leisureland
Dubai Courts
Rashid Hospital
PORT SAEED
Deira City Centre
Deira City Centre Mall

BUR DUBAI

RIYADH ROAD
Creekside Park
Khor Dubai / Dubai Creek

Children's City
Dubai Dolphinarium
Dubai Creek Marina

Dubai Creek Golf Course

J   K   L   M

Contents

ESSENTIAL DUBAI	4–18

Introducing Dubai	4–5
A Short Stay in Dubai	6–7
Top 25	8–9
Shopping	10–11
Shopping by Theme	12
Dubai by Day...and Night	13
Eating Out	14
Restaurants by Cuisine	15
Top Tips For...	16–18

DUBAI BY AREA	19–106
BUR DUBAI	20–44

Area Map	22–23
Sights	24–37
Walk	38
Shopping	39–40
Entertainment and Nightlife	41–42
Restaurants	42–44

DEIRA	45–58

Area Map	46–47
Sights	48–54
Shopping	55
Entertainment and Nightlife	56
Restaurants	57–58

NORTH SHEIKH ZAYED ROAD AND ZABEEL	59–80

Area Map	60–61
Sights	62–73
Shopping	74–75
Entertainment and Nightlife	76–78
Restaurants	78–80

JUMEIRAH AND DUBAI MARINA	81–98

Area Map	82–83
Sights	84–94
Shopping	95
Entertainment and Nightlife	96–97
Restaurants	97–98

FARTHER AFIELD	99–106

Area Map	100–101
Sights	102–103
Excursion	104
Shopping	105
Entertainment and Nightlife	105–106
Restaurants	106

WHERE TO STAY	107–112

Introduction	108
Budget Hotels	109
Mid-Range Hotels	110–111
Luxury Hotels	112

NEED TO KNOW	113–125

Planning Ahead	114–115
Getting There	116–117
Getting Around	118–119
Essential Facts	120–121
Language	122–123
Timeline	124–125

Introducing Dubai

It's difficult to imagine, but 30 years ago Dubai was a small desert town relying on trade from the Arabian Gulf. In a few busy decades, propelled by a go-getting ruling family and buoyed by oil money, it's become the business hub of the Middle East and one of the world's must-visit tourist hot spots.

The emirate of Dubai is one of seven that make up the United Arab Emirates. It raced into the 21st century with an ambitious plan to attract millions to this sunny corner of the Arabian Peninsula—the result is a glittering metropolis. The city's infectious confidence produced unique projects that stunned the world, including Burj Khalifa, currently the planet's tallest building, and the artificial Palm Islands, so big they can be viewed from space.

Sublime beaches and warm seas were a starting point, but countless dollars have been invested to make Dubai a destination of superlatives. The hotels are the most luxurious; the shopping malls the largest; you can gourmet dine at every meal. The nightlife is smoking hot, the spas ultra-cool and the recreation possibilities almost limitless. Want to ski on real snow—no problem in the heat of Dubai.

The city is amazingly multicultural. Millions of foreigners have settled to make a living, from management-level workers in the hi-tech media and financial sectors to legions of taxi drivers, waiters and housekeeping staff. However, generous Arab hospitality remains a signature of Dubai and the Emiratis who call it home. Yes, you will notice social and cultural differences, but the city has a relatively relaxed attitude to the visitors it welcomes every year.

Dubai is one of those places that polarizes opinion: if you don't enjoy a sanitized, somewhat artificial environment or the idea of whiling away hours hunting bargains or chasing a golf ball, Dubai may not be the place for you. But those who appreciate extraordinary architecture, exceptional hospitality and a bewildering choice of recreation will find Dubai more than meets their expectations.

Facts + Figures

● Population: 1.2 million in 2005; 2.2 million in 2013—of which around 300,000 are native Emiratis
● Visitors: 3 million in 2000; 10.16 million in 2012
● Hotel rooms: 80,000
● Passengers at Dubai International Airport: 65.4 million in 2013

THE UNITED ARAB EMIRATES

Dubai is one of seven emirates that together form the United Arab Emirates. The largest—economically and physically—is Abu Dhabi, which takes the lead on military and political matters. The other emirates are Sharjah, Ajman, Umm Al Quwain, Ras Al Khaimah and Fujairah. Each emirate is ruled by a family dynasty. Dubai's rulers are the Al Maktoum family.

SHEIKH MOHAMMED

Born in 1949, Mohammed bin Rashid Al Maktoum was the third son of previous ruler Sheikh Rashid. In his youth he underwent officer training in the UK. He became the head of the Dubai police force in 1968, and the first defence minister in the newly formed United Arab Emirates in 1971. He has been Crown Prince of Dubai since 1995.

EXPAT LIFE

Dubai has enticed foreign businesses by creating ultramodern infrastructure and Free Zones with long-term tax exemptions. White-collar workers enjoy tax-free salaries and perks including housing allowances, health care and free schooling for their children. No surprise then that it's a popular location to build a career or make a new life.

A Short Stay in Dubai

DAY 1

Morning Start the day at **Dubai Museum** (▷ 28), where local Emirati history and lifestyle is brought to life, then explore the neighboring Bastakiya quarter (now called **Al Fahidi Historic District**, ▷ 24) and shop for souvenirs at **XVA Gallery** (▷ 40).

Mid-morning Stop for a refreshing fruit juice at **Arabian Tea House** (▷ 43). Then take the five-minute *abra* ride across Dubai Creek and build up an appetite with a little haggling at the **Spice or Gold Souk** (▷ 50–51).

Lunch Bayt Al Waheel (▷ 43) on the Bur Dubai side overlooking the creek offers typical local cuisine with a view.

Afternoon Make your way to Sheikh Zayed Road (the Metro is quick but a taxi will be less expensive for a group) and take the lift to At The Top, the viewing platform at **Burj Khalifa** (▷ 62–63) for awe-inspiring cityscapes.

Mid afternoon To escape the last of the afternoon heat, head into **The Dubai Mall** (▷ 65), currently the largest mall in the world. Do a little shopping or visit the **Aquarium** (▷ 64).

Dinner Dine around southeast Asia in the **Umai** (▷ 80), where the open kitchen prepares a tempting range of options. At the end of the meal relax over a traditional tea ceremony.

Evening Stroll down Sheikh Mohammed bin Rashid Boulevard at **Old Town** (▷ 72) in the shadow of Burj Khalifa and watch the evening performance of **The Dubai Fountain** (▷ 66–67). Finish your evening at **Level 43** (▷ 77) at the Four Points Sheraton, currently the world's tallest hotel, with a breathtaking high-rise view of Dubai's bright lights.

DAY 2

Morning Prepare yourself with a generous breakfast. Your tour company will pick you up early for your **desert safari** (▷ 102). Leave the city far behind and head out into the dunes. This is a very different Dubai: it's an action-packed morning of high-adrenaline activities including buggy dune bashing, sand surfing and camel rides.

Lunch You'll need to recharge after an energetic morning, so head to the relaxed **Bussola on the Beach** (▷ 97–98) for a huge choice of tasty pizzas fired in a wood burning stove, and a great view of the ocean.

Afternoon Explore the alleyways and waterfront walkways of **Madinat Jumeirah** (▷ 87) with its traditional architecture. Browse the souk and take a boat ride on the canals. You can enjoy close up views of **Burj Al Arab** (▷ 86), sitting just offshore.

Mid afternoon If you have an appetite, relax over afternoon tea in the genteel surroundings of the **Al Fayrooz Lounge** (▷ 97).

Dinner Make a reservation at one of Dubai's premier tables to enjoy the Indian dishes created by Michelin-starred chef Vineet Bhatia at **Indego by Vineet** (▷ 98)—or, if your budget doesn't stretch to this, **Sim Sim** (▷ 98) in Dubai Marina is a casual café offering great local food.

Evening Stroll around the glittering towers of **Dubai Marina** (▷ 92) and take in the atmosphere at the shops, bars and restaurants of **The Walk** (▷ 92), then toast Dubai with a final drink at **360°** (▷ 96) in the shadow of Burj Al Arab, with the light show playing across its curved lines in the moonlight.

► ► ►

Al Ahmadiya School
▷ 48 Dubai's first school, founded in 1912, is now a lesson in history.

Al Fahidi Historic District (Bastakiya) ▷ 24 Dubai's last remaining historic quarter is full of traditional architecture.

Arabian Desert
▷ 102 A sea of dunes and arid plains, just outside Dubai.

Wild Wadi ▷ 91 Watery fun for all ages; prepare to get wet!

Ski Dubai ▷ 90 It's all downhill—on real snow—on the indoor slopes here, on skis, snowboards or bobsleigh.

Shindagha and the Heritage & Diving Villages ▷ 32–33 A living museum in the center of old Dubai, bringing Dubai's traditional ways back to life.

Sheikh Saeed al Maktoum House ▷ 31 Historic government palace and fine family home.

Sheikh Mohammed Center for Cultural Understanding ▷ 30 Helping forge bridges of friendship with their guided cultural tours.

Ras al Khor Wildlife Sanctuary ▷ 68–69 This salt lagoon is a vital staging post for migrating birds.

Madinat Jumeirah ▷ 87 Arabic-inspired architecture at this modern resort and entertainment complex.

Jumeirah Mosque ▷ 88–89 Elegant Islamic place of worship open to visitors by guided tour.

Hindi Lane ▷ 29 The spiritual home-from-home for Dubai's large Indian community.

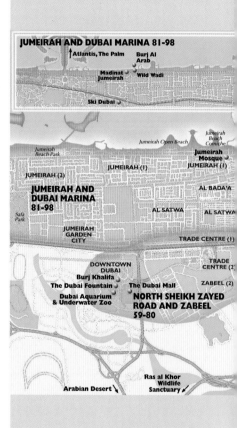

These pages are a quick guide to the Top 25, which are described in more detail later. Here they are listed alphabetically, and the tinted background shows which area they are in.

Atlantis, The Palm
▷ 84–85 Dubai's mega-resort has attractions for the whole family.

Bur Dubai Old Souk ▷ 25
From authentic chintz to kitsch clothing this bustling bazaar is packed with textiles.

Burj Al Arab ▷ 86
The world's only 7-star hotel, and a modern-day architectural icon.

Burj Khalifa ▷ 62–63
The biggest of them all, currently the tallest structure in the world.

Creekside Park ▷ 26
A green lung in the heart of old downtown.

Deira Souks ▷ 50–51
Traditional marketplaces bustling with life.

Dhow Wharves ▷ 49
Cargoes have been landed here the old fashioned way for generations.

Dubai Aquarium & Underwater Zoo ▷ 64
An awe-inspiring 10 million-litre tank stocked with more than 140 species.

Dubai Creek ▷ 27 This traditional commercial artery still throngs with trade.

The Dubai Fountain
▷ 66–67 Magnificent spouts, sprays and cascades at the world's largest choreographed water jets.

Heritage House ▷ 52
How the wealthy pearl traders of Dubai lived in the early 20th century.

Dubai Museum ▷ 28
Dubai's old fort is now packed full of dioramas and interesting history.

The Dubai Mall
▷ 65 An air-conditioned, town-sized temple to consumption.

Arabian Gulf

Pearl Jumeirah

PORT RASHID

AL SHINDAGHA

AL MINA

Shindagha and the Heritage & Diving Villages

Sheikh Saeed al Maktoum House

Heritage House

AL HUDAIBA

Bur Dubai Old Souk

Al Ahmadiya School

AL RAFFA

Deira Souks

Dubai Museum

Hindi Lane

Al Fahidi Historic District (Bastakiya)

Sheikh Mohammed Center for Cultural Understanding

AL JAFILIYA

MANKHOOL

AL HAMRIYA

AL RIGGA

AL KARAMA

Dubai Creek

AL KIFAF

RIGGAT AL BUTEEN

UMM HURAIR (1)

Dhow Wharves

Zabeel Park

ZABEEL (1)

OUD METHA

DEIRA 45–58

BUR DUBAI 21–44

UMM HURAIR (2)

Creekside Park

PORT SAEED

Dubai Creek Golf Course

◄ ◄ ◄

9

Shopping

Dubai is one of the best shopping cities in the world, and attracts an international crowd who flock to buy its high-value items. The city's traditional souks are atmospheric must-see places to explore and shop, but the city has truly embraced the air-conditioned mall—with temperatures topping 100 degrees Fahrenheit in the summer, who wouldn't? The mega-malls The Dubai Mall and Mall of the Emirates are the two stand-out venues.

Perfumes and incense

Arab culture holds scent in high regard and their perfumes are always oil based. Natural oil essences can be applied on the wrist or behind the ear, mixed with base oils for massage, and added to oil burners to scent a room. Perfume shops blend oils and package these unguents in ornate glass vessels that make ideal souvenirs. You'll find lots of different incense, along with incense burners—every Emirati home has several—but frankincense from neighboring Oman is the most prized.

Gold and jewelry

Buyers are attracted to Dubai from around the world for the exceptional prices of gold and jewelry. The price of gold is set by the international markets, but in Dubai jewelers charge less for the craftsmanship used to create the finished jewelry, plus there's no sales tax. This is why it's possible to get a bargain—especially in the Gold Souk—though jewelry shops abound.

DUBAI SHOPPING FESTIVAL

Prices across the city are slashed at the month-long sales fiesta during January and millions of dollars are given away in competitions where prizes also include supercars and apartments. A whole host of special events such as concerts expand the social calendar. More than 3 million visitors flock to the city to spend, spend, spend during the festival, and hotels in all price ranges are always full, so it pays to book ahead.

The Gold Souk; the Spice Souk; the Mall of the Emirates; Bur Dubai Old Souk; the Emirates Towers (top to bottom)

Spices

You'll find sacks piled high with saffron, pepper, turmeric, cloves, nutmeg and chili at the Spice Souk. Buy what you need by weight, or pick up ready-packaged selections of spices specially prepared for visitors.

Arabic handicrafts

From simple copper pots to ornately worked light fittings to hand-blown glass to carved wooden jewelry boxes, there's something for every room in your home.

Persian rugs

Dubai is a major importer of hand-woven Persian carpets, and prices here are lower than, say, London or New York. Most sellers will arrange export for you, so you don't need to worry about baggage allowance on the flight home.

Designer bliss

If you shop by label, you'll find paradise in Dubai. For high-value designer monikers like Giorgio Armani or Jimmy Choo the sheer concentration of big names in one place will thrill you. If your budget doesn't quite cover the high price tags, mainstream names such as Bench and Zara also have space here.

Middle-Eastern modern art

Dubai is the hub of a growing market in Middle Eastern art, particularly the work of Emirati and Persian artists. The galleries of the Al Fahidi District make a good place to start but Al Quoz close to Mall of the Emirates is developing into a locally well-known "Arts District".

BUYER BE AWARE

Dubai doesn't have VAT or sales tax, so you'd imagine that prices across the board would be cheaper than you'd pay at home. But it's not always so. Prices for designer goods are about the same as in Europe or the US. It pays to do a little research on any high-value items you intend to buy before you travel if you want to grab a bargain.

Shopping by Theme

Department stores, designer boutiques and traditional souks: you'll find them all in Dubai. On this page shops are listed by theme. For a more detailed write-up, see the individual listings in Dubai by Area.

ANIMAL THEMES

The Aquarium Store (▷ 74)
The Camel Company
(▷ 74)

ACCESSORIES

Al Washia (▷ 55)
The Cobbler (▷ 75)
Tod's (▷ 40)
Viennois Jewellery Outlet
(▷ 105)

ART

Cuadro (▷ 75)
The Empty Quarter Fine Art
Photography (▷ 75)
Gallery One (▷ 75)
Majlis Gallery (▷ 36)
XVA Gallery (▷ 40)

BOOKS

Magrudy's (▷ 95)

CARPETS

AGAS Traders (▷ 39)
Miri Creation (▷ 75)
National Iranian Carpets
(▷ 95)

CLOTHING

Bimba y Lola (▷ 39)
Bur Dubai Old Souk (▷ 25)
Folli Follie (▷ 95)
Giordano (▷ 55)
Hang Ten (▷ 55)
Hollywood Textiles
& Tailors (▷ 40)
Rinco Matching Center
& Tailoring (▷ 40)

ELECTRONICS

Jumbo Electronics (▷ 95)

FOOD

Bateel (▷ 39)
The Spice Souk
(▷ 50–51)

GOLD AND JEWELRY

Ceylon Master Gems
(▷ 74)
Chetan (▷ 74–75)
Damas (▷ 75)
The Gold Souk (▷ 50–51)
Koraba (▷ 55)
Momentum (▷ 75)

HANDICRAFTS

Al Qalm Al Zahbi (▷ 39)
Al Shareif Gallery (▷ 74)
Arabian Treasures (▷ 74)
Bab Al Funoon (▷ 39)
D.tales (▷ 95)
Fabindia (▷ 39–40)
The Handicraft Gallery
(▷ 75)
Heritage & Diving Center
(▷ 40)
Raffles Boutique (▷ 40)
Royal Dirham (▷ 40)

PERFUMES & OUDHS

Abdul Samad Al Qurashi
(▷ 74)
Ajmal (▷ 55)
Amouage (▷ 39)
The Perfume Souk
(▷ 50–51)
Swiss Arabian (▷ 55)

SHOPPING MALLS

Al Fahidi Souk (▷ 39)
Al Ghurair Mall (▷ 55)
BurJuman (▷ 39)
Deira City Center (▷ 55)
The Dubai Mall (▷ 65, 74)
Dubai Marina Mall (▷ 95)
Dubai Outlet Mall
(▷ 105)
Festival City Mall (▷ 55)
Gold and Diamond Park
(▷ 74)
Ibn Battuta Mall (▷ 105)
Mall of the Emirates
(▷ 93, 95)
Reef Mall (▷ 55)
Souk Al Bahar (▷ 74)
Souk Madinat (▷ 87, 95)
Wafi City (▷ 39)
The Walk (▷ 95)

SPORTING GOODS

Golf House (▷ 95)
Snow Pro (▷ 95)
Sun & Sand Sports
(▷ 105)

Dubai by Day …and Night

World-class leisure facilities put Dubai on the map, with golf, riding and motor racing for the active, and spas and treatments to help you chill out. The city heats up at night as the temperatures cool. It has a legendary nightlife scene, and every night is party night.

Getting active
Vast tracts of Arabian Desert have been transformed for sporting and leisure pursuits. These are a drive inland from the tourist areas, though usually no more than 30 minutes.

Relax and unwind
Wellness is big business and the best spas are impressive palaces to pleasure, usually found in luxury hotels. Less expensive day spas are located around the city.

Nightlife
Dubai's bars and clubs buzz with an international crowd and it's an ever-changing scene. A listings magazine will help you get the best out of your stay. Emiratis enjoy whiling away the evening at a café with a *shisha* (hookah or water-pipe). Many hotels have fashionable outdoor *shisha* cafés with long couches and cushions for lounging.

Night lights
Dubai is incredibly beautiful by night. Traditional architecture in Al Fahidi District, Madinat Jumeirah and Old Town glows, while the towers of north Sheikh Zayed Road and Dubai Marina dazzle. The best places for an evening stroll are along Dubai Creekside, around Dubai Marina, and on the smart new Sheikh Mohammed bin Rashid Boulevard in Old Town, Downtown Dubai.

Tour boats on Dubai Creek; a Dubai nightclub; a belly dancer entertains tourists (top to bottom)

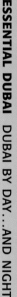

RAMADAN
During Ramadan nightlife venues may close, local shops alter their opening times, restaurants may not serve alcohol and hotels may curtail daytime food services during the month-long dawn-to-dusk fast. The three-day Eid Al Fitr festival held at the end of Ramadan is the liveliest holiday of the year for Muslims, with feasts and parties all over the city.

Eating Out

Though it's a small city, upwardly mobile Dubai has attracted some of the finest culinary talent on the planet and you'll have no trouble filling your trip with outstanding taste sensations from every continent.

Dubai in a nutshell
The restaurant scene tends to revolve around the hotels—given that Dubai has some of the finest hotels in the world, it means quality is high but it also means prices are too.

The world on a plate
The choice is vast; every culinary trend is followed and every regional cuisine has its place. Bistro and gastro pub, sushi bar and steakhouse, rest day brunch and afternoon tea, you can find it all here. Vegetarians are also well catered to, with many Middle Eastern, Asian and Indian restaurants serving delicious meat-free options.

Not just for shopping
The malls have a great range of places to eat, often with more affordable prices. You'll find contemporary and chic eateries here, with a surprising number of famous names.

Opening hours
Some upscale restaurants are open for dinner only—core hours 7–10 but often longer—but many also open for lunch around 11.30 until 3. Many mall restaurants and all cafés are open throughout the day, except during Ramadan (▷ 13).

Fine dining in Atlantis, The Palm; traditional Arabic dishes; street food in Bur Dubai (top to bottom)

DRESS CODE

In restaurants, smart casual is your guide. This means long pants and shirt for men and full sandals or shoes (not flip flops). For women most normal summer fashions are acceptable, just nothing too revealing. If you intend to wear something sleeveless or with shoestring straps, carry a shawl or light long-sleeved blouse or cardigan to slip on your shoulders when out and about.

Restaurants by Cuisine

There are restaurants to suit all tastes and budgets in Dubai. On this page they are listed by cuisine. For a more detailed description of each restaurant, see Dubai by Area.

AMERICAN-STYLE

Claw BBQ (▷ 79)
Hard Rock Café
   (▷ 57–58)
Original Wings and Rings
   (▷ 80)
Studio One (▷ 98)

ASIAN

Betawi Café (▷ 43)
Blue Elephant (▷ 57)
Creekside Japanese
   Restaurant (▷ 57)
Dapoer Kita (▷ 43)
Gypsy (▷ 44)
Hanoi Café (▷ 98)
Hoi An (▷ 79)
Karma Kafe (▷ 79–80)
Mannaland (▷ 44)
The Noodle House (▷ 80)
Umai (▷ 80)

BRITISH & IRISH

Carter's (▷ 43)
Dhow & Anchor (▷ 98)
The Irish Village (▷ 58)
The Ivy (▷ 79)
Sherlock Holmes Pub
   (▷ 44)

CELEBRITY CHEF

Carluccio's (▷ 79)
Cut (▷ 79)
Jamie's Italian (▷ 58)
Ronda Locatelli (▷ 98)
ToroToro (▷ 98)
Wheeler's of St. James
   (▷ 80)

GOURMET

Bateaux Dubai (▷ 43)
Nineteen (▷ 106)
Reflets par Pierre Gagnaire
   (▷ 58)
Table 9 (▷ 58)
Traiteur (▷ 58)

INDIAN

Amal (▷ 78)
Antique Bazaar (▷ 42–43)
Aryaas (▷ 43)
Ashiana by Vineet (▷ 57)
Gazebo (▷ 44)
Indego by Vineet (▷ 98)
Mumtaz Mahal (▷ 44)

LATIN

Cactus Cantina (▷ 43)
Café Habana (▷ 79)
Taqado Mexican Kitchen
   (▷ 80)

MEDITERRANEAN

Bice (▷ 97)
The Boardwalk (▷ 57)
Bussola on the Beach
   (▷ 97–98)
Casa de Tapas (▷ 57)
Cucina (▷ 57)
Elia (▷ 44)
Da Gama (▷ 57)
Picante (▷ 44)
Seville's (▷ 44)
Splendido (▷ 98)

MIDDLE-EASTERN

Abdel Wahab (▷ 78)
Al Bandar (▷ 42)
Al Hadheerah Arabic
   Evening (▷ 106)
Al Mallah (▷ 42)
Al Mandaloun (▷ 78)
Al Safadi (▷ 57)
Bayt Al Wakeel (▷ 43)
Local House (▷ 44)
Ottoman's (▷ 98)
Shabestan (▷ 58)
Sim Sim (▷ 98)
Zaatar W Zeit (▷ 80)
Zaroob (▷ 80)

SEAFOOD

Al Mahara (▷ 97)
Divaz (▷ 106)
Seafood Market (▷ 58)

STEAK/GRILLS

The Beach Bar & Grill
   (▷ 97)
The Big Easy Bar & Grill
   (▷ 106)
Exchange Grill (▷ 79)
The Rib Room (▷ 80)
La Parilla (▷ 98)

TEA HOUSES/CAFÉS

Al Fayrooz Lounge (▷ 97)
Arabian Tea House (▷ 43)
Dome (▷ 43–44)
La Farine Café and Bakery
   (▷ 79)

WORLD CUISINE

Fumé (▷ 98)
Spice Island (▷ 58)

Top Tips For...

However you'd like to spend your time in Dubai, these top suggestions should help you tailor your ideal visit. Each sight or listing has a fuller write-up elsewhere in the book.

ANIMAL ENCOUNTERS

Sashay across the dunes on a camel in the Arabian Desert (▷ 102).
Get a peck on the cheek from a sea lion at Sea Lion Point, Atlantis, The Palm (▷ 84–85).
Come face to face with a dolphin at Dubai Dolphinarium in Creekside Park (▷ 26).
Spot a pink flamingo on the *sabkha* at Ras al Khor Wildlife Sanctuary (▷ 68–69).
March in the snow with the penguins at Ski Dubai (▷ 90).

COCKTAILS AND DANCING UNDER THE STARS

Kick off your shoes and have your feet in the sand at Nasimi Beach at Atlantis, The Palm (▷ 97).
Rub shoulders with the Burj Al Arab at 360° Jumeirah Beach Resort (▷ 96).
Chill out under the palms on the rooftop pool deck at iKandy at the Shangri-La Hotel (▷ 77).
Arrive by boat to rock that "I'm a film star" look at 101 One&Only The Palm (▷ 96).

ISLAMIC STYLE, THEN AND NOW

Explore the alleyways of old Bastakiya in the Al Fahidi Historic District (▷ 24).
Stroll around Dubai's 21st-century homage to tradition at Old Town, Downtown Dubai (▷ 72).
Window-shop at the theme-parkesque alleyways of Souk Madinat Jumeirah (▷ 87).
Admire the neo-Fatimid monumental porch and minarets of Jumeirah Mosque (▷ 88–89).
Snap a selfie in front of the dhow-inspired curves of Burj Al Arab (▷ 86).

Meeting a dolphin; the lobby of the Burj Al Arab; local women in traditional dress (top to bottom)

Suites at Atlantis, The Palm

ROOMS WITH ATTITUDE

Sleep in ultimate luxury in a duplex suite at the Burj Al Arab (▷ 112).

Enjoy elegance personified in the world's highest building at the Armani Hotel (▷ 112).

Look out from the heart of the glass pyramid at Raffles Dubai (▷ 112).

Think big in one of the 1,500 rooms in the towering coral confection that is Atlantis, The Palm (▷ 112).

See the incredible views of Dubai's contemporary skyline from the Shangri-La (▷ 112).

CELEBRITY PLATES

Indulge in the savoir-faire of the *menu gastronomique* at Reflets by Pierre Gagnaire (▷ 58).

Savor the *cucina Italia* from Antonio Carluccio at Carluccio's (▷ 79).

Relish the refined steak at Cut by Wolfgang Puck (▷ 79).

Delight in the cultured curry of Vineet Bhatia at Indego by Vineet (▷ 98).

Revel in the zesty, tangy Latin American flavors from Richard Sandoval at ToroToro (▷ 98).

A display of decorated perfume bottles

RETAIL THERAPY

Strut down Fashion Avenue in The Dubai Mall to find all the designer names (▷ 65).

Haggle for gold and gems at The Gold Souk (▷ 50–51).

Stock up the food cupboard at The Spice Souk (▷ 50–51).

Augment your home decor at the XVA Gallery, Al Fahidi District (▷ 40).

Dubai's Gold Souk is famous for bargains on its fabulous jewelry

SWINGING THE CLUBS

Drive off at the Emirates Golf Club course, home of the Omega Dubai Desert Classic tournament (▷ 96).

Avoid the water hazards at The Address Montgomerie, designed by Colin Montgomerie, winner of eight European Order of Merit tournaments (▷ 105).

Score a hole-in-one at The Els Club course, designed by four-times major winner Ernie Els (▷ 106).

STUFF FOR KIDS

Splash around at Juha's Dhow and Lagoon, Wild Wadi (▷ 91).

Get into a snowball fight at Ski Dubai (▷ 90).

Become an airline pilot for the day at KidZania, The Dubai Mall (▷ 77).

Spin, roll and ride at Sega Republic (▷ 93).

Drive a real car at Dubai Autodrome (over 12s only, ▷ 105).

GETTING YOUR HEART PUMPING

Look down from the At The Top, 124 floors above the city at Burj Khalifa (▷ 62–63).

Plunge headlong down a nine-story drop in the Tower of Neptune at Aquaventure Waterpark, Atlantis, The Palm (▷ 84–85).

Take on the black run at Ski Dubai (▷ 90).

Snorkel with the sharks at Dubai Aquarium (▷ 64).

Kick up the sand in a dune buggy in the desert (▷ 102).

Driving off at the Emirates Golf Club; kids will love Wild Wadi; taking the plunge at Aquaventure Waterpark (top to bottom)

Dubai by Area

Sights	24–37
Walk	38
Shopping	39–40
Entertainment and Nightlife	41–42
Restaurants	42–44

BUR DUBAI

Sights	48–54
Shopping	55
Entertainment and Nightlife	56
Restaurants	57–58

DEIRA

Sights	62–73
Shopping	74–75
Entertainment and Nightlife	76–78
Restaurants	78–80

NORTH SHEIKH ZAYED ROAD AND ZABEEL

Sights	84–94
Shopping	95
Entertainment and Nightlife	96–97
Restaurants	97–98

JUMEIRAH AND DUBAI MARINA

Sights	102–103
Excursion	104
Shopping	105
Entertainment and Nightlife	105–106
Restaurants	106

FARTHER AFIELD

Nestling on the southern shores of Dubai Creek, Bur Dubai is the old settlement of the Bani Yas, the tribe of the ruling family. Splendid Arabic mansions, the city's most authentic heritage attractions and its finest historic district can be found here, all within walking distance of each other.

Sights	24–37
Walk	38
Shopping	39–40
Entertainment and Nightlife	41–42
Restaurants	42–44

Top 25 TOP **25**

Al Fahidi Historic District (Bastakiya) ▷ **24**
Bur Dubai Old Souk ▷ **25**
Creekside Park ▷ **26**
Dubai Creek ▷ **27**
Dubai Museum ▷ **28**
Hindi Lane ▷ **29**
Sheikh Mohammed Center for Cultural Understanding ▷ **30**
Sheikh Saeed al Maktoum House ▷ **31**
Shindagha and the Heritage & Diving Villages ▷ **32**

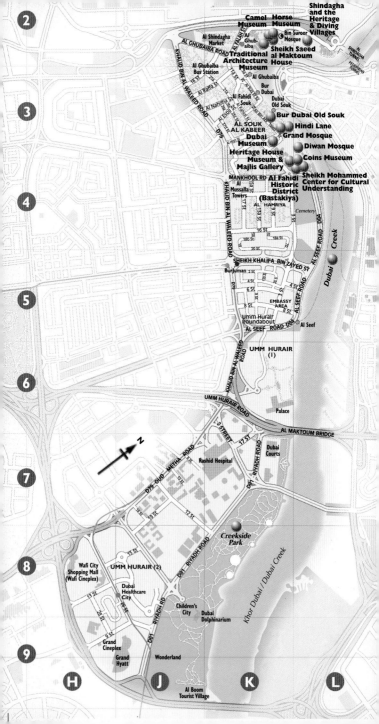

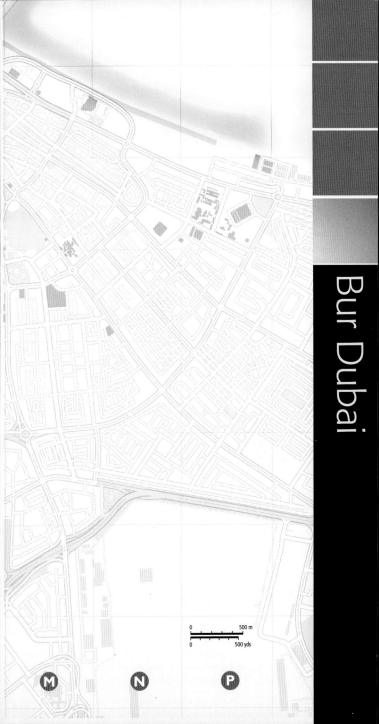

0   500 m

0   500 yds

M   N   P

Al Fahidi Historic District (Bastakiya)

TOP 25

Coffee pots displayed in the sand in Al Fahidi Historic District (left); the district lit up by night (right)

THE BASICS

www.cultures.ae

🔲 L4

✉ Al Fahidi Street

☎ 353 6666 (SMCCU)

🍴 Cafés and restaurants ($–$$)

🚇 Al Fahidi

♿ Good

🚌 Al Fahidi

HIGHLIGHTS

● Genuine old Arabic architecture
● The biggest group of old *barjeels* in Dubai
● Characterful cafés
● Fascinating galleries

TIP

● The Sheikh Mohammed Center for Cultural Understanding (▷ 30) can organize a guide if required.

Dubai's most complete traditional quarter, Al Fahidi was once an affluent neighborhood of Persian traders. This tangle of narrow alleyways is the only place in the city where you can immerse yourself in the atmosphere of old Dubai.

Al Bastakiya Al Fahidi is an early example of the shrewd forward thinking of Dubai's rulers: in the late 1800s they granted traders from the city of Bastak in Persia (modern day Iran) tax concessions and easy relocation, in much the same way as today's government encourages immigration. The traders thrived and built a quarter of impressive mansions on the creekside: Al Bastakiya.

Fall and rise By the 1960s the merchants had moved out, and Al Bastakiya nearly fell victim to the building boom. The eastern parts were demolished to make way for new offices. A visit by Prince Charles and Princess Diana in 1989 may have been its savior. Soon afterwards the surviving streets were put under a preservation order and sympathetically renovated. Al Bastakiya was renamed Al Fahidi Historic District in 2012.

Today All the buildings—around 50 in all—are made of coral walls covered with a sand plaster, and feature *barjeels*: wind towers used as an ancient form of air-conditioning. They are art galleries, museums, shops and restaurants—all subtly integrated into the historic surroundings. The neighborhood is largely car-free, which offers some respite from Bur Dubai's bustle.

Customers browsing in the souk (left and center); colorful textiles for sale in the Old Souk (right)

Bur Dubai Old Souk

One of the original market places of this erstwhile trading city, the Old Souk—also known as the Textile Souk—is one of Dubai's most energetic corners. It's a sequinned kaleidoscope of color.

Souk style This wide alleyway was covered with an arched hardwood roof in the 1990s. Myriad tiny shops fling open their merchandise-strewn doors, offering a front-of-house show worthy of a Moulin Rouge costume call. Favorites among the local expats are shimmering voiles of gold and silver thread, fashioned into colorful *saris* or *kameez*, and *pashminas* (these make a useful shoulder-cover during your stay in Dubai). Arabian kitsch is everywhere, from Sinbad-style ornate slippers, to belly-dancing outfits. The market also does a fine line in inexpensive mass-produced items, such as logo emblazoned T-shirts, *shishas* and gilded *ittar* bottles.

Serious business If you're shopping for large amounts of fabric—perhaps for curtains or business suits—this is the perfect location. You can purchase complete bolts of cashmere, silk, cotton, calico and chintz and have them shipped back home. Settle down to some serious negotiations inside the store over an Arabic coffee as the merchants bring samples for you to peruse. You can even have a dress or suit make during your stay—the tailors are extremely skilled and work fast. Also in the area is Meena Bazaar, a tight tangle of streets. There's an eclectic mixture of goods here, all at bargain prices.

THE BASICS

✚ K3
✉ Al Fahidi Historic District
🕐 Sat–Thu 9–1, 4–10, Fri 4–10
🍴 Restaurants and cafés nearby ($–$$$)
🚇 Al Fahidi
♿ Few
🚢 Dubai Old Souk

HIGHLIGHTS

● The riot of rainbow hues
● Mass produced kitsch souvenirs
● High quality inexpensive fabrics sold in any quantity

TIP

● The Textile Souk is where haggling pays dividends, especially if you are buying multiple items.

BUR DUBAI TOP 25

25

Creekside Park

The Children's City building (left); people relaxing in Creekside Park (center and right)

THE BASICS

www.dubaidolphinarium.ae

⊞ K8

✉ Riyadh Road. There are several gates accessing the park, each with a car park

☎ 336 7633 (Children's City 334 0808, Dubai Dolphinarium 336 9773)

🕐 Park: Sat–Tue, Thu 8am–11pm (Fri 8am–11.30pm women and children only); Children's City: Sat–Thu 9–8, Fri 3–9; Dubai Dolphinarium shows: Mon–Sat 11, 3 and 6

🍴 Snacks from stalls in the park ($)

♿ Good

💲 Park: inexpensive; Children's City: inexpensive; Dubai Dolphinarium show: moderate

❓ Bicycle hire from Gate 2 for additional fee

HIGHLIGHTS

● The cable-car trip
● The quiet respite from the bustling alleyways of Bur Dubai
● The dolphin shows

Creekside is the best park in Dubai, with something for everyone. A respite from the bustling streets, the views are sensational, while families will love the open space and entertaining activities.

An urban garden At 548 acres (222ha), Creekside is a very large park. Active types can explore the 1.5 miles (2.5km) of shoreline on rented bicycles, while others allow the mini-train to get them around the perimeter. Amateur horticulturalists will enjoy themed gardens containing 280 plant species. Pagodas and landscaped gardens are sequestered among the park's slopes; the desert garden features indigenous desert-dwelling plants, while the date palm grove is interspersed with traditional Arabic watchtowers. But the main attraction of Creekside Park is its cable-car system, which runs along a stretch of Dubai Creek shoreline 30m above the ground. The cars provide fantastic views of the Dubai Creek Golf & Yacht Club—an elegant building on the opposite side of the creek intended to resemble the sails of a dhow.

Fun for the young Children's City is an interactive area for kids from 2 to 15, where children can explore the world of nature, space and communications. There's a planetarium with daily shows. Dubai Dolphinarium has dolphin and seal shows throughout the day, or you can book a swim-with-the-dolphin session for adults and children over 5. There are other rather strange attractions here, including a mind-boggling Mirror Maze and a 5D/7D effects cinema.

Abra *rides on Dubai
Creek (left and center);
old wooden boats con-
trast with Dubai's mod-
ern buildings (right)*

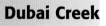

Dubai Creek

**Without the creek, Dubai would not
be what it is today. This narrow natural
inlet facilitated Dubai's development
from desert trading post to modern city.
Both aspects of Dubai still exist along
its busy banks.**

A little piece of history After the Maktoum
family settled here in 1833, Dubai slowly
prospered. The pearl-fishing industry brought
money to the port and the souks (▷ 25 and
50–51) thrived. But it wasn't until the creek
was dredged in 1960 and Abu Dhabi struck
oil, making Dubai's deep-water port essential
for importing drilling equipment, that Dubai
truly took off as an economic powerhouse.

Then… You don't have to go far to see
what life on the creek was like decades ago.
Between Maktoum Bridge and the Sheraton
Dubai Creek Hotel, Deira's creek side is awash
with wooden dhows (▷ 49), small boats
unloading everything from vegetables to TVs.

Now… The creek is lined with towers built in
the 1980s and 1990s, many housing government buildings and Dubai's first luxury hotels.
As you pass under Maktoum Bridge and the
creek widens, Creekside Park is visible, with
the impressive outline of the Dubai Creek Golf
& Yacht Club on the opposite bank. Dubai
Festival City rises ahead, then the creek curves
round to the right and broadens still farther into
the Ras al Khor lagoon (▷ 68–69).

THE BASICS

➕ L5
🍴 Numerous cafés and
restaurants ($–$$$)
♿ Few
🚤 *Abra* ride inexpensive

HIGHLIGHTS

● The *abra* ferry trip across
the creek
● The Dhow Wharves (▷ 49)
● The constant comings
and goings of wooden cargo
ships on the water

TIP

● The *abra* crossing is an
essential Dubai experience.
These narrow boats shoot
back and forth from Bur Dubai
to Deira, and from them you
can see both the modern high-
rise glass towers and the wind
towers and minarets of old
Dubai. For a longer tour, you
can rent an *abra* by the hour.

Dubai Museum

The battlements and tower of Al Fahidi Fort (left); mannequins on display in the museum (center and right)

THE BASICS

- ✚ K3
- ✉ Al Fahidi Street
- ☎ 353 1862
- 🕐 Sat–Thu 8.30–8.30, Fri 2.30–8.30, during Ramadan Sat–Thu 9–6, Fri 2–5
- 🚇 Al Fahidi
- ♿ Good
- 🎟 Free
- 🛍 Dubai Old Souk

HIGHLIGHTS

- ● The pearl-diving gallery
- ● The gallery on Bedouin lifestyle
- ● The re-creation of the Dhow Wharves
- ● The old souk area
- ● The old fort

This museum offers a fascinating journey back in time, describing life around the emirate over 5,000-years of settlement, from its trading origins to the oil boom and the current construction fever.

Al Fahidi Fort The museum is housed in a national monument, the diminutive but sturdy Al Fahidi Fort, built in the late 18th century to protect the traders and seafarers living at the mouth of Dubai's creek from invasion. You'll walk through sections re-creating traditional housing, the Dhow Wharves, the souk and the mosque, with mannequins of merchants, boat builders, potters and jewelers all setting about their everyday tasks.

Traditional Bedouin lifestyle An exhibition on the Bedouin people explains how they used their limited water supply to support their nomadic life-style and maintain the health of their camels and sheep, two animal species that were pivotal to the Bedouin's success. Another section throws light on desert ecology and how plants and animals survive average temperatures of 40°C (104°F) in summer and just 120mm (4.7 inches) of rain annually.

Pearl trade Dubai's natural pearls were prized for centuries: in the early 20th century there were about 300 pearl-diving dhows. The museum shows the rudimentary equipment used at the time when the men would make incredibly deep dives with a turtleshell clip on their noses, a 5kg (11lb) stone to pull them down, and a rope looped around their foreheads to guide them back up.

Spiritual home of Dubai's Hindu community, Hindi Lane plays host to the only Hindu Temple complex in Dubai. It's one of the most atmospheric and fragrant streets in the city, packed with stalls selling items for the *puja* (Hindu ritual prayer).

What and why Twenty-five percent of Indian expat workers are Hindu, and this narrow alleyway leading to three simple *mandhirs* (temples) to gods Shiva and Krishna, and Hindu guru Sai Baba, is always thronging with worshipers. A range of items is used during *puja,* and tiny stalls along Hindi Lane supply these in vast quantities. *Pushpam* (flower petals and garlands) decorate the statues in the temples and *dhupa* (incense cones and sticks) is burned to scent the air before the statues of the gods are bathed in milk, honey, or *ghee* (clarified butter) in an act of ritual purification. Apart from *puja* paraphernalia, look out for gaudy depictions of the major deities, such as elephant-headed Ganesh or Hanuman the monkey god, homeopathic medicines and delicious street foods.

India and Dubai Ties between India and the UAE go back hundreds of years. Today, Indians make up the largest number of expats, with some families having lived here for several generations. The community is heavily represented in the gold and textile industries, retailing and health care. In 2011 it was estimated that these workers sent $6.2 billion (£3.8 billion) back to India to support their extended families.

THE BASICS

✚ K3

✉ 62A Street, Al Fahidi Historic District

🍴 Street stalls ($)

🚇 Al Fahidi

♿ None

🚌 Dubai Old Souk

DID YOU KNOW?

The Hindu gods:
● Shiva—The Great God
● Vishnu—maintains order in the universe
● Krishna—embodiment of love
● Ganesh—god of wisdom and new beginnings
● Hanuman—monkey god, symbol of strength and perseverance
● Durga—the Mother Goddess, destroyer of evil, protector of the weak
● Kali—the dark goddess
● Lakshmi—goddess of fortune, prosperity and love
● Sarawasti—goddess of knowledge and the arts
● Rama—symbol of chivalry and virtue

BUR DUBAI TOP 25

Sheikh Mohammed Center for Cultural Understanding

TOP 25

A guide in traditional dress talks about the Muslim religion (left and center); the building's exterior (right)

THE BASICS

www.cultures.ae

⊞ L4

✉ House 26, Al Mussallah Road, Al Fahidi Historic District

☎ 353 6666

🕐 Sun–Thu 8–6, Sat 9–1

🚇 Al Fahidi

♿ Good

👄 Cultural tours and meals moderate

ℹ Cultural tours: 60-minute tours Sun–Thu 9am, 90-minute tours Sun, Tue, Thu 10.30am, Sat 9am; Cultural meals: breakfast Mon, Wed 10am, lunch Sun, Tue 1pm, dinner Tue 7pm; Jumeirah Mosque tour: Sun–Thu 10am

🚌 Al Fahidi

HIGHLIGHTS

● The opportunity to interact with native Emiratis in a social atmosphere

● The chance to learn about the Bedouin roots of the Bani Yas tribe

● Exploring the current lifestyle of your Emirati hosts

Founded by the current Sheikh in 1998, the aim of the center is to increase cross-cultural understanding in this multicultural corner of the world, under the motto "Open doors. Open minds".

Cultural tours The center offers a number of guided tours that will enhance your understanding of Dubai history and Emirati society. You can take a 60-minute or 90-minute tour of Al Fahidi Historic District (old Bastakiya, ▷ 24). Both these tours offer background information about the traditional architecture and the longer tour, also called the Heritage Tour, includes a visit to nearby Diwan Mosque (▷ 34).

Cultural meals Enjoy a range of traditional local foods with an informative Emirati host who'll be happy to answer any questions that you have about his Bani Yas tribe, Islam and Emirati lifestyle and customs. Advance booking is required. You don't need to book to take the Jumeirah Mosque tour (▷ 88–89). Just be at the mosque at 9.45am.

Emirati national dress Emiratis have a distinctive national dress. Men wear a *kandura* (known in Dubai as a *dishdasha*), a full-length sleeved light coat of white cotton, with a *kaffiyah* (white cotton headdress), held in place by an *agal* (a light rope). Women wear the *abaya*, a long, black, loose-fitting light coat. Their hair is covered with a *hijab* that wraps around their neck. The *niqab* (face veil) is not required, though some women choose to wear it.

Sheikh Saeed al Maktoum House

The exterior of the house (left); a traditional barjeel *(wind tower, center); detail of a door (right)*

This exceptional Arab mansion, the house and *majlis* of former ruler Sheikh Saeed al Maktoum, is now a museum documenting Dubai's transition from desert state to skyscraper city through a collection of fascinating black-and-white photographs.

Sheikh Saeed Grandfather of the current prince, Saeed ruled from 1912 until his death in 1958. His reign was a challenging period for Dubai, with economic crisis brought on by the collapse of the pearl trade in the 1920s when Japan discovered how to create cultured pearls. He didn't live to see the discovery of oil in the region, dying the same year that the fields were first confirmed.

The house This is classical Emerati architecture on the grandest scale. Constructed over two stories in 1896 from coral covered in lime and sand plaster, the region's traditional building technique, its myriad rooms are today decorated with high-quality rugs and period furniture. *Majlis* means meeting place in Arabic—but Saeed's meetings were much more than a simple get together. This was the epicenter of power during Saeed's reign, where he held court, made decisions and issued edicts.

The collections Two wings of the house display photographs offering fascinating views of Dubai through the last century. The Marine Wing charts the end of the old ways with images of the last pearl divers, while the Al Maktoum Wing documents the birth of Dubai's technological age.

THE BASICS

✚ K2

✉ Waterfront, Shindagha

☎ 393 7139

🕐 Sat–Thu 8am–8.30pm, Fri 3pm–8.30pm; during Ramadan Sat–Thu 9–5, Fri 2–5

🚍 Al Ghubaiba

♿ Good

💷 Inexpensive

🚤 Al Ghubaiba

HIGHLIGHTS

● The *majlis*, the meeting room of state
● Exquisite hand-crafted furniture
● Photographs of the pearl-diving community
● Images of a Dubai of yesteryear in the mid to late 1900s

TIP

● Philatelists will love the collections of postage stamps, including those issued by the Trucial States (precursor to the United Arab Emirates) from 1853 to 1971.

BUR DUBAI TOP 25

Shindagha and the Heritage & Diving Villages

THE DIVING VILLAGE

HIGHLIGHTS

● Being enveloped in the atmosphere of the desert camp
● Your chance to come face-to-face with a camel
● A close encounter with a trained falcon
● Sipping traditional sweet mint tea while sitting around the fire

Immerse yourself in the Dubai of the past and dive into the traditional Bedouin lifestyle of the Arabian Desert without leaving the city, at the most important living museum in the emirate.

The district One of the oldest districts in Dubai, Shindagha became home for the ruling family's Bani Yas tribe when they left their Bedouin lifestyle behind at the beginning of the 20th century.

Bedouin traditions The village itself is set in a huge courtyard. As you enter you'll see a clutch of *barasti* (diminutive thatched huts) that signal the Bedouin village; a faithful interpretation of the desert camp, with real people re-enacting how generations of the Bani Yas lived. Their camels wait patiently and sheep lie quietly in their pens. While

The Heritage & Diving Villages in Bur Dubai chart the history of pearl diving, which at one time was the major industry of Dubai

the women sit weaving and make Arabic sweets in a pot atop the fire, the men are busy metal working or preparing their falcons for the hunt.

Diving for pearls Pearls were the economic lifeblood of Dubai for several generations, but diving to find the valuable gems was dangerous, with men reaching depths of 40m (130ft) with no breathing apparatus. The Diving Village re-creates the Creek waterfront of this era, showing the divers getting ready to set out on a diving trip, mending equipment and repairing their boats.

When to visit Evenings are the best time to visit, as the restaurant serves traditional Emirati dishes and local families come to enjoy the cool air, with the kids playing in the sand and the men relaxing over *shisha*.

THE BASICS

✚ L2

✉ Shindagha waterfront

☎ 393 7139

🕐 Sat–Thu 8.30am–10pm, Fri 3.30–10. During Ramadan Sat–Thu 9am–2pm and 8.30pm–midnight, Fri 8.30pm–midnight

🚇 Al Ghubaiba

♿ Few

💷 Free

🚢 Shindagha

More to See

CAMEL MUSEUM

Built in the 1940s close to Sheikh Saeed al Maktoum's house, this building was designed as a camel stables, so it's a fitting location for the museum. Several rooms are filled with well-presented information about the importance of these "ships of the desert" to Bedouin society. How does the camel survive so well in these arid climes? You'll find out here as you look into the stomach of a model camel, hump and all. But perhaps the most fun exhibit here is the surround-effect re-creation of a camel race, complete with the sound of an enthusiastic crowd, where you can climb aboard a life-size model and ride your animal to victory.

🔲 K2 ✉ Shindagha ☎ 353 9265 ⏰ Sun–Thu 8–2 🚇 Al Ghubaiba ♿ Few 💷 Free 🚌 Al Ghubaiba

COINS MUSEUM

Converted into a museum in 2004, this old Al Bastakiya mansion now displays almost 500 rare and valuable coins dating from as far back as the Rashidun Caliphate c.632 AD, minted just after the Prophet Mohammed's death. Other interesting examples come from around the Arab world, including Fatimid, Mamluk and Ottoman examples. A specialist interest, perhaps—but the quality of the collection makes it a must for amateur numismatists.

♿ L4 ✉ By Al Farooq Mosque, Al Fahidi Historic District ☎ 353 9265 ⏰ Sun–Thu 8–2 🚇 Al Fahidi ♿ Few 💷 Free 🚌 Al Fahidi

DIWAN MOSQUE

Built in 1990 as the mosque for the Diwan or government buildings to which it's attached, the Diwan Mosque occupies a prime area of Dubai Creek waterfront. The whole complex is Mamluk Islamic in design, in homage to the architectural style developed during the rule of the Mamluk dynasty across the Arab world, c.13th–16th centuries.

🔲 L3 ✉ Al Musalla Roundabout, Al Fahidi Historic District 🚇 Al Fahidi

Coins Museum

Close-up of an Arabic coin

Few 📱 By guided tour only, through the Sheikh Mohammed Center for Cultural Understanding (▷ 30) 🚇 Al Fahidi

GRAND MOSQUE

Dubai's largest mosque hides itself away among the cluster of streets in the heart of the souk district in Bur Dubai. Standing on the site of an original 1900 building, the present mosque dates from the late 1990s and is rather unassuming in design. The Anatolian-style minaret—looking much like a lighthouse tower—is the tallest in the city at 70m (230ft). Take up a position nearby as the call to prayer echoes and you'll see the faithful arriving from all directions, leaving lines of shoes outside and entering the mosque barefoot, as is the Islamic custom.

✚ K3 ✉ Al Fahidi Historic District ☎ 392 0368 🕐 Not open to non-Muslims 🚇 Al Fahidi 🚻 None 🚇 Dubai Old Souk

HERITAGE HOUSE GALLERY

Built in 1925 and renovated in 2006, this traditional Emirati mansion now houses the exhibition rooms of the Alserkal Cultural Foundation. The main aim of the foundation is the showcasing and promotion of regional arts and culture. An ever-changing programme of exhibitions concentrates on Emirati and Gulf states artists and traditional cultural forms, while the foundation provides space for study and for Emirati youth to explore their native art forms.

✚ K4 ✉ Al Fahidi Historic District ☎ 353 5922 🕐 Sat–Thu 9–9 🚇 Al Fahidi 🚻 Few 🚻 Free 🚇 Al Fahidi

HORSE MUSEUM

This small museum explores the importance of the Arabian stallion in the traditional Arab lifestyle. The house was built in the 1940s, one of the last great mansions in the district, and owned by a female member of the Al Maktoum family. She created the museum during her lifetime. There's a lot here for horse lovers to explore, from the history of the Arabian breed to traditional horse care in the desert.

Worshipers in front of the Grand Mosque

🔲 K2 ✉ Sheikha Mozah Bint Saeed House, Shindagha ☎ 392 0368 🕐 Sun–Thu 8–2 🚇 Al Ghubaiba ♿ Few 🎫 Free 🚌 Al Ghubaiba

MAJLIS GALLERY

www.themajlisgallery.com

Expat Alison Collins fell in love with Dubai and the traditional architecture of Al Bastakiya. When she arrived, the arts scene was as dry as the desert, and the gallery functioned as a meeting place and much-needed showcase for the arts community. Since then, Majlis has developed into one of the premier galleries in the UAE. The building itself, an old mansion with rooms set around a traditional courtyard, is worth a visit, but it's the range of art mediums on show, combined with Alison's knowledge of art and her artists, that make it a must for any prospective purchaser.

🔲 K4 ✉ Al Musalla Roundabout, Al Fahidi Historic District ☎ 353 6233 🕐 Sun–Thu 10–6, closed Jul 31–Sep 6 🚇 Al Fahidi ♿ Good 🎫 Free 🚌 Al Fahidi

TRADITIONAL ARCHITECTURE MUSEUM

Built in 1927 as the home of Sheikh Juma bin Maktoum, this large mansion is a prime example of fine Islamic and Arabic design. The informative museum functions on two levels. Firstly, it explores and explains traditional Arabic and Islamic design, showing the forms and patterns used by architects—relating to window details and arches over doors and entrance portals. Secondly, there are dioramas of traditional building methods, with mannequins of builders and plasterers at work using the materials, tools and methods of traditional construction, and explanations of the customs behind these. Of special interest is how these methods have been used to renovate the buildings in Shindagha and in the Al Fahidi Historic District (▷ 24).

🔲 K2 ✉ Shindagha District ☎ 392 0093 🕐 Sun–Thu 8–2 🚇 Al Ghubaiba ♿ Good 🎫 Free 🚌 Al Ghubaiba

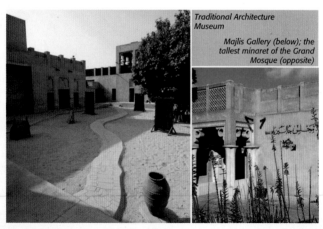

Traditional Architecture Museum

Majlis Gallery (below); the tallest minaret of the Grand Mosque (opposite)

Bur Dubai District

Bur Dubai is one of the oldest neighborhoods in the city and the most rewarding to explore on foot. Its key sights, strung along the creek, bring Dubai's history to life.

DISTANCE: 1.8 miles (3km) **ALLOW:** 5 hours with stops

START

HERITAGE & DIVING VILLAGES ✚ L2

① Start from the Heritage & Diving Villages (▷ 32–33) at the mouth of the creek. Explore the re-creation of a traditional Bedouin desert camp and a pearl diving village before moving on.

② Keeping the creek on your left, you walk only a few hundred meters before you see Sheikh Saeed al Maktoum House (▷ 31) on your right. This is a fine example of traditional architecture with an interesting collection of photographs of old Dubai.

③ Continue to follow the creek around to the left until you reach the Bur Dubai *abra* station. It's always busy with people here. Turn right, then left into the covered alleyway of the Old Souk (▷ 25). Inside the souk you will pass stalls selling clothes, snacks, fabrics and souvenirs.

END

AL FAHIDI HISTORIC DISTRICT (BASTAKIYA) ✚ L4

⑦ At the end of Al Fahidi Street, before the roundabout, you'll arrive in Al Fahidi Historic District (▷ 24). This is the largest area of old traditional architecture in the city. Explore the alleyways and wind towers, browse the Majlis Gallery (▷ 35) and stop for refreshments at Arabian Tea House (▷ 43) next door.

⑥ After exiting the museum, turn left along Al Fahidi Street, crossing a small intersection to join a strip of neon-lit shops.

⑤ Before you pass the mosque turn right, away from the creek and uphill. The Dubai Museum (▷ 28) in the Al Fahidi Fort is ahead. The entrance is on the far side, past a ship used for pearl diving, called a *sambuk*.

④ Continue until you reach the end of the souk and the Grand Mosque (▷ 35), which has the tallest minaret of any mosque in Dubai, at 70m (230ft).

Shopping

BUR DUBAI MALLS

Bur Dubai's main malls are the Egyptian-themed Wafi City (www.wafi.com) in Oud Metha, and BurJuman (www.burjuman.com) with its plethora of haute-couture names. Air-conditioned Al Fahidi Souk opened in mid-2014 to provide more souvenir-style shopping close to the Old Souk.

AGAS TRADERS

www.wafi.com
With trading contacts throughout the Gulf and westward to Turkey and the Kurdish region, AGAS offers an excellent collection of hand-made carpets and rugs complemented by a small but high-quality selection of antiques and handicrafts.
⊞ H8 ⊠ Murjan Souk, Wafi City Mall, Oud Metha ☎ 327 9780 🕐 Sat–Wed 10–10, Thu–Fri 10am–midnight 🚇 Dubai Healthcare City

AL QALM AL ZAHBI

www.wafi.com
Islamic calligraphy is an art form, and Amir Hossein Golshani exquisitely engraves or carves it on materials like wood, leather and stone, and in silver or gold filigree. He can also engrave in English.
⊞ H8 ⊠ Murjan Souk, Wafi City Mall, Oud Metha Road ☎ 050 252 2537 🕐 Sat–Wed 10–10, Thu–Fri 10am–midnight 🚇 Dubai Healthcare City

AMOUAGE

www.amouage.com
This upscale store sells *ittars* and blends different oils to produce a range of exclusive off-the-shelf perfumes, as well as bath products and home fragrances.
⊞ H8 ⊠ Wafi City Mall, Oud Metha ☎ 324 3135 🕐 Sat–Wed 10am–10pm, Thu–Fri 10am–midnight 🚇 Dubai Healthcare City

BAB AL FUNOON

www.wafi.com
A small gallery with a fine collection of antiques and handicrafts from around the Arab world. This is not mass-market, but one-of-a-kind pieces—perfect for finding that showpiece holiday souvenir.
⊞ H8 ⊠ Murjan Souk, Wafi City Mall, Oud Metha ☎ 327 9727 🕐 Sat–Wed 10–10, Thu–Fri 10am–midnight 🚇 Dubai Healthcare City

DUBAI SUMMER SURPRISES

Younger sibling of Dubai's immense Dubai Shopping Festival discount-fest held during January, Dubai Summer Surprises (www.summerisdubai.com) is specifically scheduled to pump up visitor numbers during the uncomfortably hot summer season. Running from mid-June to early September, the discounts of up to 75 percent have proved a big hit with spenders, who don't need to worry about the outdoor temperatures—they just head to the air-conditioned malls, where it's temperate 24 hours a day all year round.

BATEEL

www.bateel.com
Bateel is renowned for its upscale grocery products. Best buys are the dried dates, date cookies and chocolates—all beautifully packaged. There are several outlets around the city.
⊞ K5 ⊠ BurJuman Center, Khalid bin al Waleed Road at corner of Trade Center Road ☎ 355 2853 🕐 Sat–Wed 10am–10pm, Thu–Fri 10am–11pm 🚇 BurJuman

BIMBA Y LOLA

www.bimbaylola.com
Spanish-designed young, fun clothing and accessories including colorful handbags—these are trendsetters.
⊞ K5 ⊠ BurJuman Center, Khalid bin al Waleed Road at corner of Trade Center Road ☎ 352 2030 🕐 Sat–Wed 10–10, Thu–Fri 10am–11pm 🚇 BurJuman

FABINDIA

www.fabindia.com
This is a one-stop-shop for clothing, textiles and homewares produced in India. Almost everything on sale is made by hand using traditional techniques. It's a huge modern air-conditioned store,

which makes it a delight to explore.

⊞ H3 ✉ Nashwan Building, Al Mankhool Road, Mankhool ☎ 398 9633 ⏰ Sat–Thu 10–10, Fri 4pm–10pm

HERITAGE & DIVING CENTER

This tourist attraction sells traditional Bedouin folk art and handicrafts, some of which are made onsite. There's a good range of local pottery and small woven items.

⊞ L2 ✉ Shindagha waterfront ☎ 393 7139 ⏰ Sat–Thu 8.30am–10pm, Fri 3.30pm–10pm. During Ramadan Sat–Thu 9am–2pm and 8.30pm–midnight, Fri 8.30pm–midnight ⍾ Al Ghubaiba

HOLLYWOOD TEXTILES & TAILORS

www.hollywooduae.com
This long-standing tailors will sell you the fabric, measure you and run you up a suit in 48 hours. They also sell accessories such as ties and cufflinks.

⊞ K3 ✉ 25 C Street, Old Souk, Al Souk Al Kabeer ☎ 352 8551 ⏰ Sat–Thu 9.30–1.30 and 4–10, Fri 6pm–9pm ⍾ Al Fahidi

RAFFLES BOUTIQUE

www.raffles.com
Branded items from this upscale hotel chain—towels, bathrobes and clothing, along with a selection of souvenirs from locations where Raffles have their hotels.

⊞ H8 ✉ Wafi City Mall,

Oud Metha ☎ 314 9544 ⏰ Sat–Wed 10–10, Thu–Fri 10am–midnight ⍾ Dubai Healthcare City

RINCO MATCHING CENTER & TAILORING

One of the best places to get your prom or bridal gown made. Take a pattern or a picture and choose the fabric—they have a huge range of finishes and colors. It'll only take a couple of days. They'll also make Indian traditional clothing to your size.

⊞ K3 ✉ Cosmos Lane, Meena Bazaar, Al Souk Al Kabeer ☎ 050 744 9930 ⏰ Sat–Thu 9.30am–10.30pm, Fri 4.30pm–10.30pm ⍾ Al Fahidi

ROYAL DIRHAM

Lovers of the kitsch, gauche and garish will

KARAMA MARKET

For rock-bottom prices on mass-market products like last season's electricals and clothing, head to the alleyways of Karama Market, set around the Al Karama Shopping Center. Be careful though—fake designer items are rife here and the Dubai authorities have periodic crackdowns on importers and sellers. Counterfeit goods can look just like the real thing but they are illegal, so if there are any doubts about authenticity check before you buy.

adore the selection of mass-market souvenirs and Indian trinkets on sale here, from jewel-encrusted camels to phallic Burj Khalifa miniatures: and all at the lowest prices in the city.

⊞ K4 ✉ Al Musalla Road, Mankhool ☎ 355 4331 ⏰ Sat–Thu 10–10, Fri 4.30pm–10pm ⍾ Al Fahidi

TOD'S

www.tods.com
Among a wealth of designer names in this classy mall, Tod's sells the best in high-quality leather shoes and accessories. The epitome of understated Italian elegance, they'll make great long-term staples for your wardrobe.

⊞ K5 ✉ BurJuman Center, Khalid bin al Waleed Road at corner of Trade Center Road ☎ 355 4417 ⏰ Sat–Wed 10–10, Thu–Fri 10am–11pm ⍾ BurJuman

XVA GALLERY

www.xvagallery.com
Opened in 2003, this gallery/café/hotel is one of the stalwarts of Al Bastakiya with an inventive program of exhibitions and art on sale. The Design Shop has a huge range of decorative arts, clothing and jewelry. XVA Gallery also has exhibition space at Gate Village in the Financial District close to Sheikh Zayed Road (▷ 71).

⊞ L4 ✉ Al Fahidi Historic District ☎ 353 5383 ⏰ Daily 10–6 ⍾ Al Fahidi

Entertainment and Nightlife

AHASEES SPA & CLUB

www.dubai.grand.hyatt.com

A private and relaxing spa with plunge pools, sauna, steam room and Jacuzzi.

➕ J9 ✉ Grand Hyatt Hotel, Umm Hurair (2) ☎ 317 1234 🕐 Daily 9–9 🚇 Dubai Healthcare City, Al Jadef

AL BOOM TOURIST VILLAGE

www.alboom.ae

Nine dhows set off from Al Boom every evening for cruises down Dubai Creek; prices include onboard dining, with a range of traditional dishes.

➕ J9 ✉ Umm Hurair (2), next to Garhoud Bridge ☎ 324 3000 🕐 Late-night cruises 10.30pm–midnight

AL NASR LEISURELAND

www.alnasrll.com

An aging complex with a bowling alley, ice-skating rink and tennis and squash courts. Regular upgrades and show events mean its popularity endures.

➕ J7 ✉ Umm Hurair Road, Oud Metha, near the American Hospital ☎ 337 1234 🚇 Oud Metha

CLASSIC ROCK COFFEE

www.classicrockcoffee.com

A new concept café combining freshly ground coffee and classic rock. Guns N'Roses' Ron Thal is behind the whole thing and played a gig to open the venue. There are regular live sessions.

➕ J8 ✉ Building 33, Dubai Healthcare City, Umm Hurair (2) ☎ 050 656 0113 🕐 Daily 7am–10pm 🚇 Dubai Healthcare City

CLEOPATRA'S SPA

www.cleopatrasspaand wellness.com

The theme at this spa is ancient Egypt, although the hammam-like wet room has Mediterranean influences. Guests can access the Pharaoh Club's swimming pool.

➕ H8 ✉ Wafi City, Oud Metha ☎ 324 7700 🕐 Women daily 9–9; men (separate door) Sun, Thu 10–9.30, Fri 10–9 🚇 Dubai Healthcare City

THE ENCOUNTER ZONE

www.wafi.com

This huge indoor children's entertainment and activity center puts action at the heart of the fun. For older children, there's a paintball arena, a skateboard track, and The Tomb House of Horrors, a ride full of scary antics. Younger kids will enjoy the ropes and tunnels in Crater Challenge.

➕ H8 ✉ Wafi City, Oud Metha ☎ 324 7747 🕐 Sun–Wed 10–10, Thu–Fri 10am–midnight 🚇 Dubai Healthcare City

THE MUSIC ROOM

www.themusicroomdubai.com

Live music is the key draw here, with a resident band, KaPOW!, and a regular guest program.

➕ J4 ✉ Majestic Hotel, Mankhool Road ☎ 50 248 4054 🕐 Daily 6pm–3am 🚇 Al Fahidi

NOVO CINEMAS

www.grandcinemas.com

12-screen cinema complex close to Wafi City Mall and Creekside Park.

➕ J9 ✉ Umm Hurair (2), near Grand Hyatt Hotel ☎ 324 2000 🚇 Dubai Healthcare City

PEOPLE BY CRYSTAL

www.raffles.com

Ultra-cool lounge occupying the top two floors of the glass pyramid at the Raffles Hotel. Great views and fashionable crowds.

➕ H8 ✉ Raffles Dubai, Wafi City, Oud Metha ☎ 324 8888 🕐 Thu–Sat 11pm–3am 🚇 Dubai Healthcare City

THE PULSE

www.movenpick-hotels.com

www.pulsedubai.com

Black leather and stainless steel decor set the scene at this club, which spins a range of house, techno, R&B, hip hop and

THE BAR SCENE

Dubai's bar scene changes rapidly. Today's hip bar will be tomorrow's has-been, although some places are so swanky they seem to be immune from this syndrome. For the very latest tips on what's hot or not, use an online listings directory such as www.platinumlist.net or the Wednesday entertainment supplement of the *Gulf News*.

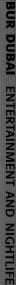

retro sounds. Women and couples get in free.
➕ H7 ✉ Mövenpick Hotel, 19th Street, Oud Metha ☎ 358 2090 🕐 Daily 7pm–3am 🚇 Dubai Healthcare City

SPIN

http://dubai.spingalactic.com
The USP here is the ping-pong tables. Spin caters to an eclectic crowd, with *shisha*, food and an outdoor terrace.
➕ H8 ✉ Pyramids, Wafi City, Oud Metha ☎ 370 7707 🕐 Sat–Wed 6pm–1am, Thu–Fri 6pm–3am 🚇 Dubai Healthcare City

VINTAGE WINE BAR

www.pyramidrestaurants atwafi.com
A cosy wine bar with an endearing lack of snobbery. The wine list covers most of the world. Also hosts fondue nights (Sun).
➕ H8 ✉ Pyramids, Wafi City, Oud Metha ☎ 324 4100 🕐 Fri–Wed 6pm–1.30am, Thu 4pm–2am 🚇 Dubai Healthcare City

WONDER BUS

www.wonderbusdubai.net
Wonder Bus travels on land and on water for a unique perspective of Dubai's

streets and the creek.
➕ K5 ✉ BurJuman Center, Khalid bin al Waleed Road at corner of Trade Center Road ☎ 55 511 7936 🕐 Daily, reservation required 🚇 BurJuman

WONDERLAND DUBAI

www.wonderlanduae.com
Wonderland, at Garhoud Bridge, encompasses a water park, Splashland, with slides and rides, and a funfair.
➕ J9 ✉ Riyadh Road, Umm Hurair (2) ☎ 324 1222 🕐 Daily 10am–midnight, water-park daily 10–8 🚇 Al Jadef

Restaurants

AL BANDAR ($–$$)

Set in the living heritage village, this atmospheric restaurant offers delicious local cuisine. For the most part it's simple fare but good value. It's a popular place for Emiratis to enjoy a late-evening into early-hours *shisha*.
➕ L2 ✉ Heritage & Diving Villages, Bur Dubai creek side, Shindagha ☎ 393 9001

🕐 Lunch, dinner 🚇 Al Ghubaiba

AL MALLAH ($)

This simple cafeteria-style eatery offers the best *shwarmas* around. It's a great place to fill up if you

are on a budget and a chance to mix with the expats who come for the home-style cooking.
➕ F4 ✉ Al Dhiyafa Road, Satwa ☎ 398 4723 🕐 Breakfast, lunch, dinner. Closed Fri breakfast

ANTIQUE BAZAAR ($–$$)

www.antiquebazaar-dubai.com
One of Dubai's best Indian restaurants, Antique Bazaar attracts a devoted Asian clientele with excellent food and a comprehensive list of dishes. This is not the best place for a quiet tête-à-tête, though.
➕ K3 ✉ Four Points by

Sheraton Bur Dubai, Khalid Bin al Waleed Road ☎ 397 7444 ⊙ Lunch, dinner, closed Fri lunch 🚇 BurJuman

ARABIAN TEA HOUSE ($)

www.arabianteahouse.co
An essential pit stop on any tour of old Bur Dubai. Super snacks, such as the souk salad of couscous, chicken, cashew and lettuce, seem perfectly matched to the tranquil surroundings. The juice bar serves several delicious blends.

✚ L4 ✉ Al Musalla-Al Fahid roundabout, Al Fahidi Historic District ☎ 353 5071 ⊙ Lunch, dinner 🚇 Al Fahidi

ARYAAS ($)

www.aryaasgourmet.com
You'll find some of the best Indian food around at this two-story restaurant. The interior is modern and contemporary but the menu sticks to well-loved staples at an excellent price.

✚ K5 ✉ Bank Street, opposite BurJuman Mall, Al Hamriya ☎ 357 7800 ⊙ Breakfast, lunch, dinner 🚇 BurJuman

BATEAUX DUBAI ($$$)

www.jaresortshotels.com
Contemporary fine dining is only part of the appeal here. The food is excellent but this sleek modern boat with full-sized glass windows also sets out on a sedate trip along Dubai Creek as you are served with your meal.

✚ L4 ✉ Dubai Creek, Al Hamriya ☎ 814 5553 ⊙ Dinner 🚇 Al Ghubaiba

BAYT AL WAKEEL ($)

With a shady terrace jutting out over the waters of Dubai Creek there's no better place for lunch with a view. The food is authentic and local, with a selection of fresh fish served as you like. Service is variable.

✚ K2 ✉ Close to Bur Dubai *abra* station, Al Ghubaiba ☎ 353 0530 ⊙ Lunch, dinner 🚇 Al Ghubaiba

BETAWI CAFÉ ($)

A modern colorful café serving arguably the best Indonesian food in the city. It's a casual and bustling place, especially in the evenings. The food is delicious.

✚ J5 ✉ Shop 20–21 Mabrooka 1 Building, Street 4B, Al Karama ☎ 759 8118 ⊙ Breakfast, lunch, dinner (open 24 hours) 🚇 Abu Dhabi Commercial Bank (ADCB)

BRUNCH

Brunch on Friday mornings is a Dubai institution. The beginning of the Islamic weekend is the signal for visitors and expatriates to settle down to sumptuous buffets and glasses of chilled champagne at hotel restaurants across the city. The preferred spots are at beachfront hotels, but most hotels will offer some sort of brunch deal.

CACTUS CANTINA ($$)

www.cactuscantinadubai.com
For the tastiest margaritas, a choice of aged tequilas and authentic Mexican dishes you can't beat this eatery, where cantina menu meets contemporary decor.

✚ H8 ✉ Pyramids, Wafi City, Oud Metha ☎ 357 4441 ⊙ Lunch, dinner 🚇 Dubai Healthcare City

CARTER'S ($$)

www.pyramidsrestaurants
atwafi.com
This modern British-style bar offers a menu based around English pub food. There's an English roast brunch every Friday and English Premier League games on the big screens.

✚ H8 ✉ Pyramids, Wafi City, Oud Metha ☎ 324 4100 ⊙ Lunch, dinner 🚇 Dubai Healthcare City

DAPOER KITA ($)

www.dapoerkita.com
Dapoer Kita means "our kitchen" in Indonesian, and this basic cafeteria-style eatery is where you'll sit alongside Indonesian expats enjoying excellent authentic dishes.

✚ H5 ✉ Sheikh Mohammed Building, 43 A Street, Al Karama ☎ 379 5501 ⊙ Lunch, dinner 🚇 Abu Dhabi Commercial Bank (ADCB)

DOME ($)

www.domeuae.com
Weary shoppers refuel with coffee, cakes and snacks at this café. Decor is mock-French, with wait-

ers in black-and-white uniforms and dinky berets.

 K5  BurJuman Center, Khalid bin al Waleed Road at corner of Trade Center Road  355 6004  Breakfast, lunch, dinner  BurJuman

ELIA ($–$$)

www.dubaimajestic.com
Greek food with a modern twist by celebrity chef Yiannis Baxevanis. Inventive contemporary dishes match Mediterranean staples such as Greek salad and tzatziki.

 J4  Majestic Hotel, Mankhool Road  501 2666  Dinner  Al Fahidi

GAZEBO ($)

www.gazebo.ae
Great Indian food with excellent service. Tandoori-cooked meats are a specialty, as are the biriyanis, and you can eat well for less than 80 AED.

 H3  Kuwait Road, Mankhool  359 8555  Lunch, dinner

GYPSY ($–$$)

www.gypsychinese.com
Well-produced Chinese cuisine by a restaurateur who's been in business since the 1980s.

 J4  Grand Excelsior Hotel, Kuwait Road, Mankhool  653 2004  Lunch, dinner

LOCAL HOUSE ($)

www.localhouse.net
You can find out what camel tastes like at this traditional Arabic restaurant. Main dishes are competitively priced.

 L4  Al Musalla-Al Fahid roundabout, Al Fahidi Historic District  353 2288  Lunch, dinner  Al Fahidi

MANNALAND ($–$$)

If you're missing your regular dose of *kimchi* (pickled cabbage), head to this simple Korean café. The menu explains what the dishes are—the marinated ribs are excellent—and the Korean expat clientele tell you it's authentic.

 F3  Al Mina Road, Satwa, Al Hudaiba  345 1300  Lunch, dinner

MUMTAZ MAHAL ($)

www.mumtazmahalrestaurant.com
Dishes from the northwest of India and Mughlai are served in a colorful yet refined dining room. There's a varied choice of vegetarian and fish dishes, and live music.

BUDGET OPTIONS

Follow the legions of blue-collar expat workers to the Al Karama district for bottom-dollar, no frills, but ultra-authentic Lebanese/Emirati, Indian, Thai and Indonesian eateries. They'll often be quiet early in the evening but, as the clock races towards midnight, the tables will be packed with a buzzing crowd. Don't expect to pay by credit card—these places usually operate on a cash-only basis.

 K3  Arabian Courtyard Hotel, Al Fahidi Street  351 9111  Lunch, dinner  Al Fahidi

PICANTE ($$)

www.picantedubai.com
Though it serves decent steaks and European staples, you really need to visit Picante for its Portuguese specialties. The seafood *cataplana* and chicken *estufado* are delicious.

 K3  Four Points by Sheraton Bur Dubai, Khalid Bin al Waleed Road  397 7444  Lunch, dinner  Al Fahidi

SEVILLE'S ($$)

www.pyramidsrestaurants atwafi.com
For entertainment with your tapas, try Seville's, where a flamenco guitarist serenades diners. On winter evenings, as the cocktails flow, the atmosphere can become positively Balearic.

 H8  Pyramids, Wafi City, Oud Metha  324 4777  Lunch, dinner  Dubai Healthcare City

SHERLOCK HOLMES PUB ($–$$)

www.arabiancourtyard.com
This is a typical old-style English pub popular with expats, serving beer and pies, grills and burgers, with sport on the TV and regular live bands.

 K3  Arabian Courtyard Hotel, Al Fahidi Street  351 9111  Lunch, dinner  Al Fahidi

Deira

North of Dubai Creek, Deira is a densely populated old commercial and administrative quarter, bigger on bustle and atmosphere than pretty views. Close to the creek mouth you'll find a cluster of attractions, including some of the most vibrant and economically buoyant souks in the Middle East.

Sights	48–54	Top 25	TOP 25
Shopping	55	Al Ahmadiya School ▷ 48	
		Dhow Wharves ▷ 49	
Entertainment		Deira Souks ▷ 50	
and Nightlife	56	Heritage House ▷ 52	
Restaurants	57–58		

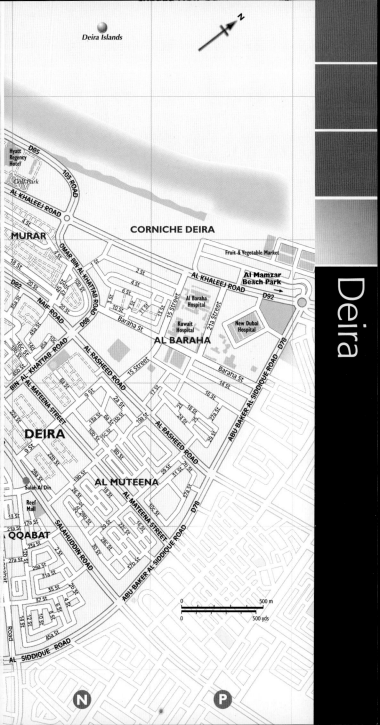

Al Ahmadiya School

Decorated arches in the Al Ahmadiya School (left); interior of a classroom (center); looking over a balcony to the courtyard (right)

THE BASICS

🚇 L3

✉ 28 Sikka Street

☎ 226 0286

🕐 Sat–Thu 8am–8.30pm, Fri 2pm–8.30pm; during Ramadan Sat–Thu 9am–4.30pm, Fri 2.30pm–4.30pm

🚇 Al Ras

♿ Poor; steps to upper floor

🎫 Free

🛍 Deira Old Souk

HIGHLIGHTS

● Authentic dioramas of 1920s schooling as it used to be
● Photos of the Al Maktoum family through the generations

TIP

● Combine a visit to Al Ahmadiya School with neighboring Heritage House (▷ 52).

Dubai's first school, Al Ahmadiya catered to the children of the elite. Even rulers studied in these simple classrooms: Sheikh Rashid bin Saeed al Maktoum, Prince of Dubai from 1958 to 1990, was educated here.

The birth of the education system The school first opened in 1912, funded by Sheikh Mohammed bin Ahmed bin Dalmouk, a wealthy pearl merchant. The initial phase consisted of a single story, set round an open courtyard. Demand soon outstripped capacity, so the upper floor and *barjeel* were added between 1920 and 1922. At its peak, occupancy rose to 300 pupils but by 1963 the number of students had outgrown its premises and they were relocated. The school was renovated in 1995. Life-size models occupy desks in the formal classrooms where calligraphy, mathematics, literature and astronomy were taught, and sit cross-legged around the Al Muttawa, or religious teacher, learning the Koran by rote.

Education in the UAE Even as the first oil was being pumped out of the desert, the Emirates had no structured education system. There were just 20 schools across the country, catering to around 4,000 students—all boys. When the UAE was formed in 1971, one of its first acts was to formalize education and create a compulsory system through ages 4 to 17. Today the UAE government provides free education for boys and girls through to university level. Literacy rates are measured at 98 percent for men, 96 percent for women.

Traditional wooden dhows (left and center); men loading cargo at the Dhow Wharves (right)

TOP 25

Dhow Wharves

Dubai Creek was once one long wharf where dhows would moor up and disgorge their cargoes. Today only a short section remains, but it's a colorful and lively location that provides a snapshot of the past.

When is a dhow not a dhow? Technically the boats that land their cargoes here today are not dhows (Arabic sail boats)—the square-hulled vessels that line up here are all motorized. Still, their wooden hulls and decks hark back to days gone by, having changed little in the last few decades.

Navigating where? Trade from the dhow wharves is mostly bound for local ports. Most of the workaday vessels make short hops across to Iran, around the peninsula to Oman and Yemen, or down the coast of the Indian subcontinent, with a nine- or ten-day turnaround in Dubai for unloading and loading—by hand. There are mountains of goods stacked along the quayside, everything from baby food to air-conditioning units. It's an amazing insight into how much of the world's sea transport is still low-tech and labor intensive.

On the deck Set under the high-rise towers of Deira waterfront, this is not an area set up as a tourist attraction. With small cranes and lifting equipment constantly on the move, you'll need to pay attention. But it's a gritty, real location where you can chat with crews who love English Premier League soccer clubs and like to practise their English. You may just be invited to come aboard for a refreshing mint tea and tour of the vessel.

THE BASICS

L6
Deira Waterfront, accessed from Baniyas Road
None
Baniyas

HIGHLIGHTS

● The old-style wooden vessels
● Old working practises long lost at mechanized container ports
● The amazing range of products heading into and out of the city
● Interaction with nationalities not normally on the tourist radar

TIPS

● If venturing onto the wharves wear comfortable shoes and dress modestly.
● A friendly hello ("as-salamu alaykum" in Arabic) breaks the ice.

DEIRA TOP 25

Deira Souks

THE BASICS

➕ L3

✉ Spice Souk: Al Ras waterfront; Perfume Souk: off Balidiya Street; Gold Souk: Al Khor Street

🕐 All souks Sat–Thu 9–1, 4–10, Fri 4–10

🚊 Al Ras

♿ Good

🚢 Deira Old Souk

TIPS

● Haggling is compulsory if you don't want to overpay.
● In the evening, the Gold Souk is a great place for people-watching.

Deira's street markets forged Dubai's reputation as an international trading post, selling high-value goods from around the region. Today, little appears to have changed.

The Gold Souk The Gold Souk grew up in the 1940s and this lattice of streets is today lined with more than 300 shops selling gold jewelry. Endless window displays shimmer with millions of dollars-worth of precious metal. And if you don't like any of the bling on offer, a craftsman can create a piece to your design in a couple of days.

The Perfume Souk The shops of the Perfume Souk are reputed for their range of *ittars*. These are perfume oils produced from natural sources such as flowers or herbs, and can be used

Transporting goods in Deira; dried foodstuffs in the Spice Souk; spices; masses of jewelry on sale in the Gold Souk; Deira by night; shopping for gold (clockwise from left)

singly or blended. You can even create your own unique fragrance for its pleasing aroma or homeopathic benefits. You'll also find incense in its natural forms—rock, crystal, wood, and resin—or processed in the form of cones and sticks.

The Spice Souk Goods aren't limited to spices: peppercorns, cinnamon, cloves and nutmeg are in abundance, but you'll also find frankincense, camomile tea, rose petals, dried chilies and lemons. The best buys are vanilla pods and saffron.

The Covered Souk What would have at one time been Deira's main general market is now a riot of mundane but essential items from pots and pans to brooms and dustpans. Perhaps not a place to shop for souvenirs but certainly a chance to see a slice of everyday life, Dubai-style.

DID YOU KNOW?

● Oil-based *ittars* don't contain alcohol like modern western perfumes.
● One drop is enough to perfume your body.
● Body heat intensifies the scent.
● *Ittar* lasts 10 times longer than alcohol-based perfume, can be stored for years and doesn't degrade.

Heritage House

Dioramas in the Heritage House

THE BASICS

➕ L3
✉ 28 Sikka Street
☎ 226 0286
🕐 Sat–Thu 8–7.30, Fri 2.30–7.30; during Ramadan Sat–Thu 9–5, Fri 2–5
♿ Poor; steps to upper floor
✋ Free
🚇 Deira Old Souk

HIGHLIGHTS

● The women's *majlis*
● The shaded *barasti* in the courtyard
● The clay water-storage jars and other kitchenalia

Explore how Dubai's well-to-do inhabitants lived in the last century; room by room, Heritage House explains everyday life in a typical Emirati family home between 1890 and the 1950s, before the arrival of domestic electricity in the 1960s.

History It was built in 1890 by Mattar bin Saeed bin Muzaaina and was bought by pearl trader Sheikh Mohammed bin Ahmed bin Dalmouk (who funded Al Ahmadiya School) in 1910. It passed into the hands of Ibrahim al Said Abdullah in the 1930s before the Dubai government, recognizing its value as a window on an era only just vanished, bought and renovated it in the 1990s.

How to explore The house is set over two floors with an outside courtyard, with each room presented exactly as it would have been when in use as a family home. Life-size models depict typical activities. The museum ranks as the most informative in Dubai, with displays explaining what every item in the room was used for.

The heart of the family home The *majlis* is the heart of an Emirati house. It's the room for receiving visitors and, since hospitable Arab families welcomed friends and strangers alike, it is usually separate from the living quarters. Women had their own *majlis* where they could entertain female family and friends—a display in the Heritage House shows the household's women sewing, making Arabic coffee and applying henna to their hair.

AL MAMZAR BEACH PARK

In an urbanized area, the 90ha (222-acre) Al Mamzar Beach Park is a pleasant open space offering four beaches and several green swaths of land, chalets, barbecue and picnic areas, and playgrounds. The beach areas have changing facilities and sunbeds, and you can rent jet skis to zip through the deeper waters away from the swimming zones. If you'd rather not bathe in the sea, the park has swimming pools with lifeguards on duty, or you can take a trip around on a rented bike or enjoy a little-train ride (very popular with families on a hot Sunday afternoon). The large amphitheater hosts regular events, and there are fields for sports including athletics and basketball, plus activity areas for children. You can also rent a chalet for the day.

✚ Off map at P4 ✉ Deira Corniche beyond Al Himriya Port ☎ 296 6201 🕐 Sun–Wed 8am–10pm, Thu–Sat 8am–11pm Ⓑ Excellent Ⓜ Inexpensive, swimming pool inexpensive

DEIRA ISLANDS

www.nakheel.com

The plans for Palm Deira were announced at the height of Dubai's building frenzy, an offshore island like Palm Jumeirah (▷ 93), reaching 12.5km (7.5 miles) into the gulf. The infrastructure was intended to be in place by 2013, and by the end of 2007, 300 million cubic metres (10.6 billion cubic feet) of sand had been used to raise the base from the seabed—30 percent of the total area of the initial plan. Then came the 2008 world financial crisis. Funding dried up as the property markets crashed, and the Palm Deira project was put on hold. It wasn't until 2013 that developers Nakheel announced a revamped plan under the name Deira Islands, and the cranes and construction equipment are once again on the move offshore. There's little to see just yet but expect more shopping, hotels, beaches and entertainment complexes when complete.

✚ N2 ✉ Off Deira Corniche ☎ Developer: 390 3333 🚇 Palm Deira

Al Mamzar Beach Park

More to See

DUBAI MUNICIPALITY MUSEUM

Built in 1957 to house the offices of Dubai Municipality, the building was converted into a museum in 2006. In addition to its administrative role, the building operated as a classic *khan* or *han*, with commercial premises set below a dormitory for traders who arrived by sea to service the souks. Today the lower floor houses several shops selling tourist souvenirs, while the upper floors display artifacts relating to the development and running of the city.

➕ L3 ✉ Baniyas Road, on Dubai Creek ☎ 225 3312 🕐 Sun–Thu 8–2 🚇 Al Ras ♿ Few ♨ Free 🛍 Deira Old Souk

DEIRA FISH MARKET

This long-standing market is a Deira institution for locals, where fish from around the region is sold in commercial quantities and to individual customers. Obviously, as they day goes on, it gets grittier, with several tons of fish being gutted and skinned—so if you are a little squeamish about this, make a visit early.

➕ M3 ✉ Al Khaleej Road, Deira Corniche ☎ 353 9265 🕐 Daily 8–1.30 and 4–11 🚇 Palm Deira ♿ Few ♨ Free

NAIF MUSEUM

Naif Fort was in a sense the changing of the guard in terms of Dubai's architecture. Constructed in 1939 during the reign of Sheikh Rashid as the first HQ of the Dubai Police Force and jail, its first tower section was in the classical defensive style. Restored in the 1990s, it's now a small museum relating to the history of Dubai law enforcement, from its formation in 1956. The first police chief was the current Sheikh, who took on the role at the age of 19. Photographs show him in his youth with a force that numbered in the single digits. Other exhibits include old uniforms and weapons, plus several short videos.

➕ M3 ✉ Sikkat al Khail Road, Naif ☎ 226 0286 🕐 Sun–Thu 8–7.30, Fri 2.30–7.30 ♿ Good ♨ Free

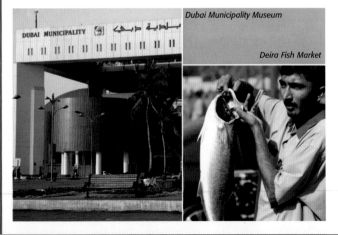

Dubai Municipality Museum

Deira Fish Market

Shopping

DEIRA MALLS

The north bank of the creek has two large malls. Deira City Center (www.deiracitycenter.com) is the oldest large mall and the styling is less dramatic than others but it's still a shopping mainstay. Festival City Mall (www.dubaifestivalcity.com) is beautifully designed and anchored by a large Marks & Spencer. Closer to the heart of downtown is Reef Mall (www.reefmall.com) and newly renovated Al Ghurair Mall (www.alghuraircentre.com). There are neighborhood malls in every district.

AL WASHIA

www.alwashia.com
Sells tasteful-to-gaudy hair and gown accessories and jewelry set with a variety of zirconium and crystal gems for that special occasion, plus everyday-wear necklaces and bangles.
L8 Deira City Center Mall, Baniyas Road, Port Saeed 295 0221 Sat–Wed 10am–midnight, Thu–Fri 10am–1am Deira City Center

AJMAL

www.ajmalperfume.com
Founded in 1951, Ajmal now has over 300 fragrances on their portfolio and supplies concentrated *ittars* (oils) and *eau-de-parfums* in beautifully crafted bottles. They also offer high-quality Oudh oil—the most expensive oil in the world.

L8 Deira City Center Mall, Baniyas Road, Port Saeed 295 3580 Sat–Wed 10am–midnight, Thu–Fri 10am–1am Deira City Center

GIORDANO

www.giordano.com
Simple easy-to-wear fashions from this chain, founded in Hong Kong in 1971, that now has stores all across the Asia Pacific region—cotton slacks, shirts, jeans and T-shirts all at reasonable prices. There are several stores across the city.
N5 Reef Mall, Salahuddin Road, Al Muraqqabat 228 8570 Sat–Wed 10am–11pm, Thu–Fri 10am–midnight Salahuddin

HANG TEN

www.hangten.com
The original surf-clothing brand, Hang Ten began the sport-brand genre in the 1960s and today produces ranges of clothing and accessories for action sports (bike, skate and surf) that look equally cool for casual lifestyle and sightseeing. Other outlets can be found in malls around the city.
Off map Century Mall, Al Wuheida Road, Al Mamzar 296 6452 Sat–Wed 10am–11pm, Thu–Fri 10am–midnight

KORABA

www.koraba.com
Jewelers based in Dubai with a large selection of items in gold, and a gem-studded range. Their specialty, however, is high-quality amber pieces, with resin imported from Poland. Other stores around the city.
Off map Festival City Mall, Dubai Festival City 435 5655 Sun–Wed 10am–10pm, Thu–Sat 10am–midnight

SWISS ARABIAN

www.swissarabian.com
Gulf-based company who work with Swiss perfumiers to produce a wide range of fragrances in concentrated oil or lighter sprays.
L8 Reef Mall, Salahuddin Road, Al Muraqqabat 223 2140 Sat–Wed 10am–11pm, Thu–Fri 10am–midnight Salahuddin

Entertainment and Nightlife

AEROGULF SERVICES

www.aerogulfservices.com
Get an unparalleled bird's-eye view of Dubai on a (pricey) helicopter tour.
✚ Off map ✉ Dubai International Services, Garhoud Road, Garhoud ☎ 877 6120 ⏱ Reservations required

AMARA SPA

www.dubai.park.hyatt.com
Each room at this Moroccan-themed resort has a private garden with a refreshing rain shower. The spa also has an 80ft (25m) swimming pool.
✚ K8 ✉ Park Hyatt Dubai, Port Saeed ☎ 602 1234 ⏱ Daily 9am–10pm

BALLOON ADVENTURES EMIRATES

www.ballooning.ae
The company's large balloons can carry up to 40 people and be booked for groups or individuals. Flights take off in time for the sunrise.
✚ Off map ✉ Pick up from your hotel or from meeting place at the IKEA/Plug In car park at Dubai Festival City ☎ 285 4949 ⏱ Oct–May daily

BEYOND EL RANCHO

www.marcopolohotel.net
Live music from the resident band, DAMAGE, as well as a resident DJ keeps this relaxed eatery/entertainment venue buzzing all evening. The food is Tex-Mex and the signature margarita is a must.

✚ N5 ✉ Marco Polo Hotel, Al Muteena Street, Al Muteena ☎ 272 0000 ⏱ Daily 7pm–3am 🚇 Salah Al Din

HIBIKI KARAOKE LOUNGE

www.dubai.hyatt.regency.com
With over 10,000 songs to choose from, there's sure to be something to suit your style. Resident singer Pocholo performs to warm the audience up.
✚ M3 ✉ The Galleria, Hyatt Regency Hotel, D85 Deira Corniche ☎ 317 2222 ⏱ Mon–Sat 7.30pm–3am

ICE SKATING RINK

www.dubai.hyatt.regency.com
There are regular sessions on the ice here, or lessons are available. You can hire skates, but you'll need to bring socks or buy some at the rink.

ALCOHOL

You'll notice that all Dubai's bars and clubs are in hotel complexes. This is because these are the only places licensed to sell alcohol. Dubai treads a thin line between welcoming Western tourists and their boozy habits and respecting the Islamic tenets of abstinence. There are a few ground rules. Do not consume alcohol in the streets or behave drunkenly outside nightspots. Once inside a bar, you will find all forms of alcohol widely available.

✚ M3 ✉ The Galleria, Hyatt Regency Hotel, D85 Deira Corniche ☎ 209 6550 ⏱ Mon–Sat 10–12.30, 1–3.30, 4–6.30, 7–10; Sun 10–12.30, 1–4.30, 5–9.30

IFLY

www.theplaymania.com/ifly
Learn to skydive indoors at this fun attraction where you balance belly-down on a chute of air, just a couple of feet off the ground. Tuition for first-timers is included in the price.
✚ Off map ✉ City Center Mall, Mirdif ☎ 231 6292 ⏱ Sun–Wed 10am–11pm, Thu–Sat 10am–midnight 🚇 Deira City Center

MAKATI COMEDY AND SING ALONG BAR

www.asianahoteldubai.com
Popular with the growing Pinoy and Pinay expat population from the Philippines, this is one of the few venues in the city to see or perform stand-up.
✚ N5 ✉ Asiana Hotel, Salahuddin Road, Al Muraqqabat ☎ 238 7777 ⏱ Mon–Sat 7pm–3am 🚇 Salahuddin

VOX CINEMAS

www.voxcinemas.com
This multi-screen complex has a newly installed 4DX system, including the effects of rain, fog, wind and lightning in the auditorium, to enhance the viewing experience.
✚ L8 ✉ Deira City Center Mall, Baniyas Road, Port Saeed ☎ 600 599905 🚇 Deira City Center

Restaurants

AL SAFADI ($–$$)

www.alsafadi.ae
In this huge courtyard complex with outside dining and an air-conditioned dining room you'll find well-cooked uncomplicated Lebanese/local dishes.
M6 ⊠ Al Rigga Road, Al Muraqqabat ☎ 227 9922 Lunch, dinner Al Rigga

ASHIANA BY VINEET ($$$)

www.ashianadubai.com
High-class Indian cuisine by Dubai's Michelin starred Indian chef, this is a sumptuous wood-panelled dining venue.
L5 ⊠ Sheraton Dubai Creek Hotel and Towers, Baniyas Road, Riggat al Buteen ☎ 207 1733 Lunch, dinner; closed lunch Fri–Sat Union

BLUE ELEPHANT ($–$$)

www.blueelephant.com
A longstanding favorite, this Thai restaurant has elaborate traditional decor—you cross a bridge over a carp pond to get to your table—and the food works well, with a menu of well-chosen dishes.
M8 ⊠ Al Bustan Rotana Hotel, Casablanca Road,

Garhoud ☎ 282 0000 Lunch, dinner. Closed dinner Tue

THE BOARDWALK ($$)

www.dubaigolf.com
Mediterranean-style dishes in an idyllic setting on the creek with downtown vistas. The deck is a wonderful place for lunch, but this place comes alive in the evening.
L8 ⊠ Dubai Creek Golf & Yacht Club, Garhoud ☎ 295 6000 Lunch, dinner; breakfast Fri–Sat

CASA DE TAPAS ($)

www.casadetapas.ae
This funky bar is an excellent place for Spanish tapas, with a good choice of hot and cold varieties for snacks or meal building. They also serve tasty portions of paella.
L8 ⊠ Dubai Creek Golf & Yacht Club, Garhoud ☎ 416 1800 Lunch, dinner

CENTURY VILLAGE

Century Village (www.centuryvillage.ae) is a large alfresco restaurant complex behind the Aviation Club in Garhoud. There are nine venues to choose from, including Da Gama (see right), with menus from India to Japan to Italy. As the tables fill up around the huge terrace there's a great atmosphere. It's a popular place for the weekend crowd.

CREEKSIDE JAPANESE RESTAURANT ($–$$)

www.creeksidejapanese restaurant.com
There's a full range of Japanese cuisine at this smart café, with cooking stations for sushi, noodle or wok cooking, and teppanyaki amongst others.
L5 ⊠ Sheraton Dubai Creek Hotel and Towers, Baniyas Road, Riggat al Buteen ☎ 207 1750 Dinner Union

CUCINA ($–$$)

www.marriott.com
Delightful Italian trattoria with authentic styling and mouth-watering pizzas cooked in a wood-burning stove, along with tasty pastas and to-die-for risottos.
N6 ⊠ JW Marriott Hotel, Abu Bakr Al Siddique Road, Al Khabaisi ☎ 262 4444 Lunch, dinner Abu Bakr Al Siddique

DA GAMA ($$)

Named after the Portuguese explorer Vasco da Gama, you'll find a selection of this country's favorite recipes, as well as a choice of Mexican dishes.
M9 ⊠ Century Village, The Aviation Club, Garhoud ☎ 282 3636 Lunch, dinner

HARD ROCK CAFÉ ($–$$)

www.hardrock.com
A taste of America at this well-known chain, with a long list of burgers,

Restaurants

smokehouse ribs and chicken, plus full-to-the-brim sandwiches.
🔹 Off map ✉ Festival City Mall, Dubai Festival City ☎ 232 8900 🕐 Lunch, dinner

THE IRISH VILLAGE ($–$$)

www.theirishvillage.com
For almost 20 years, the best in Irish hospitality and hearty food has been served up here, and it isn't just the Irish expats who return time after time.
🔹 L9 ✉ Off 2nd Street, Garhoud ☎ 239 5000 🕐 Lunch, dinner 🚇 GCICO

JAMIE'S ITALIAN ($$)

www.jamieoliver.com
Jamie Oliver's relaxed style comes to Dubai at this Italian eatery. The menu isn't extensive, but the pasta is made fresh daily and the pizzas are baked in a wood-burning stove—delicious.
🔹 Off map ✉ Festival City Mall, Dubai Festival City ☎ 432 9969 🕐 Lunch, dinner

REFLETS PAR PIERRE GAGNAIRE ($$$)

www.pierre-gagnaire.com
The chef has a bag full of Michelin stars to his name, so expect high quality and innovation from a Pierre Gagnaire menu. Exciting French flair abounds.
🔹 Off map ✉ Intercontinental Dubai, Dubai Festival City ☎ 701 1111 🕐 Dinner

SEAFOOD MARKET ($$–$$$)

www.lemeridien-dubai.com
Set out like a market stall, this is a simple concept. Choose your fish or seafood from the selection on display and the chef will cook and serve it as you like.
🔹 M9, off map ✉ Le Meridien Dubai, Garhoud ☎ 217 0000 🕐 Lunch, dinner 🚇 Airport Terminal 3

SHABESTAN ($$)

www.radissonblu.com
Iranian restaurant Shabestan serves aromatic breads, kebabs and other Persian classics. Live music adds to the Arabic experience, and the interior has a lavish sultan's palace theme.
🔹 L4 ✉ Radisson Blu Hotel, Deira Creek, Baniyas Road ☎ 222 7171 🕐 Lunch, dinner

---

THE *SHWARMA*

The *shwarma* is the fast-food of choice in Dubai and in the downtown districts of Deira and Bur Dubai you'll find stall after stall selling this delicious street food. Thin slices are carved from cooked meat rotating on a rotisserie and this is packed into flatbread with salad and hummus, and the whole thing tightly wrapped in paper. Pick these up to quash the hunger pangs for around 30 AED.

SPICE ISLAND ($$)

www.ihg.com
Multiple cooking stations offer a trip around the world at this all-you-can-eat buffet. It's particularly busy at Friday brunch. There are over 200 dishes to choose from so it's a great family option—though perhaps not for the indecisive.
🔹 N6 ✉ Crowne Plaza Hotel, Salahuddin Road, Al Muteena ☎ 262 5555 🕐 Breakfast, lunch, dinner 🚇 Salah Al Din

TABLE 9 ($$$)

www.table9dubai.com
One of the Middle East's most innovative dining concepts, the team here create original and ever-changing menus with classical style. The six-course vegetarian tasting menu offers non-meat-eaters a rare option, an upscale well-balanced series of dishes designed to compliment each other.
🔹 L6 ✉ Hilton Dubai Creek, Baniyas Road, Riggat Al Buteen ☎ 212 7551 🕐 Dinner

TRAITEUR ($$$)

www.dubai.park.hyatt.com
The closest cooking gets to theater in Dubai is at Traiteur, where nine chefs prepare modern European-style dishes in an open kitchen. The Friday brunch is one of the best in the emirate.
🔹 K8 ✉ Park Hyatt Dubai, Port Saeed ☎ 317 2222 🕐 Dinner, Fri brunch

The modern city first burst out of its confines at the top of Sheikh Zayed Road, the main artery leading south towards Abu Dhabi. Today, this strip is business central, and it offers the emirate's most striking architecture, coolest hotels and classiest dining, shopping, and entertainment options.

Sights	62–73	Top 25	TOP 25
Shopping	74–75	Burj Khalifa ▷ 62	
		Dubai Aquarium &	
Entertainment		Underwater Zoo ▷ 64	
and Nightlife	76–78	The Dubai Mall ▷ 65	
		The Dubai Fountain ▷ 66	
Restaurants	78–80	Ras al Khor Wildlife	
		Sanctuary ▷ 68	

North Sheikh Zayed Road and Zabeel

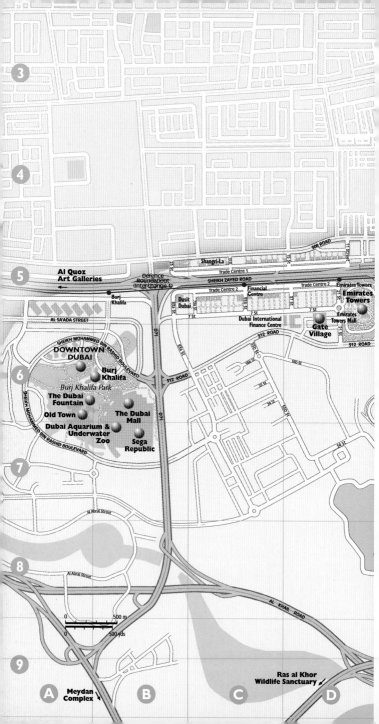

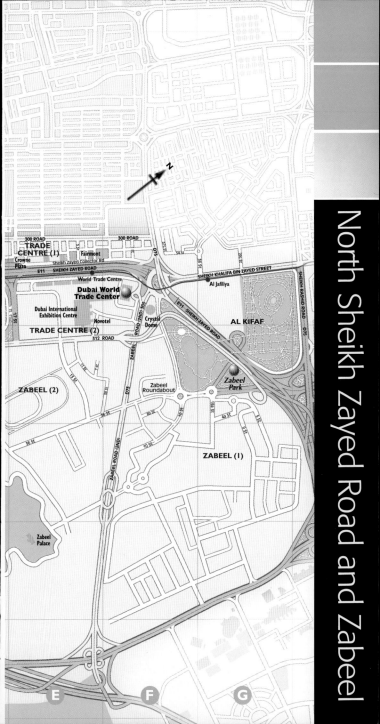

308 ROAD
308 ROAD
TRADE
CENTRE (1)
Fairmont
Crowne
Plaza
Sheikh Zayed Collector Rd
E11 SHEIKH ZAYED ROAD
World Trade Centre
SHEIKH KHALIFA BIN ZAYED STREET
Dubai World
Trade Center
Al Jafiliya
Dubai International
Exhibition Centre
Novotel
Crystal
Dome
AL KIFAF
TRADE CENTRE (2)
312 ROAD
ZABEEL (2)
Zabeel
Roundabout
Zabeel
Park
ZABEEL (1)
ZABEEL ROAD 2ND)
D75
Zabeel
Palace

E   F   G

Burj Khalifa

The tallest building in the world shoots arrow-like 825m (2,716ft) into the sky above Dubai, a graceful needle of aluminum and glass. It's the most astounding structure in the city, and perhaps the world.

Planning Architect Adrian Smith found inspiration for the Y-shaped base of the tower in a desert flower's petals. The triple-lobed shape helps resist the region's strong winds, while an outer layer of reflective panels withstands the ferocious heat of the Dubai summer. The project broke ground in 2004 and the tower was inaugurated in 2010.

The community Burj Khalifa was not simply meant to be an impressive status symbol; it was designed as a vertical community. There are 900 apartments serviced by fitness centers

Local women in traditional burka robes on the observtion deck at the Burj Khalifa; the world's tallest building; Downtown Dubai at dawn, the Burj Khalifa prominent; information panels inside the entrance to the building (clockwise from left)

and swimming pools, shops and a library, and even an 11ha (27-acre) garden. Visitors are no less pampered, with a luxury boutique hotel designed by Giorgio Armani (▷ 112) with eight restaurants and a 12,000sq ft (1,100sqm) spa.

At The Top The operators of Burj Khalifa have installed an amazing visitor attraction offering an exhilarating adrenalin rush and truly jaw-dropping views whatever the time of day. At The Top observation deck sits 124 stories above the ground, and as soon as the lift door opens you'll be assaulted by 360° uninterrupted views all across Dubai. For a VIP experience (at extra cost), At The Top SKY is 24 stories higher and your own Burj Khalifa "ambassador" will accompany you on a personal tour of what is currently the world's highest public access space.

THE BASICS

www.burjkhalifa.ae

➕ B6

✉ Near Interchange 1, Sheikh Zayed Road. Entrance to At The Top from basement level in The Dubai Mall (▷ 65)

☎ 888 8124 or in Dubai 800 2884 3867 (800 AT THE TOP)

🕐 At The Top Daily 10–10

🍴 On-site restaurants, cafés, bars, At The Top Sky Café

Ⓜ Burj Khalifa/Dubai Mall

♿ Excellent

💰 At The Top expensive

❓ Audio guide inexpensive

Dubai Aquarium & Underwater Zoo

Lion fish at Dubai Aquarium & Underwater Zoo (left); an observation tunnel (right)

THE BASICS

www.thedubaiaquarium.com

🔲 B7

🖂 Ground Floor, The Dubai Mall, Financial Center Road, off Sheikh Zayed Road

☎ 342 2993

🕔 Sun–Wed 10–10, Thu–Sat 10–midnight

🚇 Burj Khalifa/Dubai Mall

🚻 Very good

🎫 Various ticket packages available starting moderate

HIGHLIGHTS

● The feeling that you're part of the ocean world
● All those sharp teeth at shark feeding time
● King Croc

TIP

● You can have your underwater experiences recorded on film at extra cost.

The towering acrylic walls of this impressive 10 million-gallon tank create an interface between our world of air and the world of water. It's as if a slice of the ocean has been teleported here—fish and all.

Vital stats Over 140 species, including more than 300 sharks and rays, glide around the 51m-long, 20m-wide and 11m-high space. A walk through the acrylic tunnel gives you a surround-sensation effect as they swim over the top of you. The daily feeding sessions up the action, with scuba-clad aquarium staff feeding by hand. The fish get fed at 7.30pm, rays at 10am and 2pm and the sharks at 4pm.

Experiences There are several "experiences" to add on to the basic trip. The glass-bottom boat ride is the most sedate, but cage snorkeling and the shark walk—in the cage wearing an oxygenized helmet—put you right at the heart of the action. Spending the day with a keeper, feeding the sharks and other fish with a qualified staff member, is ideal for amateur naturalists.

Not just sealife King Croc is a 40-year-old saltwater crocodile from Queensland, Australia. He's already 5m (16ft) in length and weighs 750kg (1,600lb) and is considered one of the biggest captive crocodiles in the world—and he hasn't finished growing! Another gallery re-creates nighttime in the desert wadis and dunes, showing a selection of Dubai's nocturnal animals you'd probably never see otherwise.

There's plenty of shopping to be done in The Dubai Mall

The Dubai Mall

Shopping heaven or shopping hell, The Dubai Mall has over one million square metres of air-conditioned retail space with more than 1,200 shops. It's the biggest combined shopping and entertainment complex on earth.

Fashion avenue If you want to prioritize haute couture brands, make your way straight to Fashion Avenue, on the east side of the mall overlooking the lake, where the latest season offerings by Laboutin, Hermès and Max Mara amongst others are there to tempt you.

DubaiDino The Dubai Mall's newest attraction is the skeleton of a *Diplodocus longus*, a dinosaur discovered in Wyoming, USA in 2008. Dubai's "dino" is 24m (80ft) long and 7.6m (25ft) high and weighed the same as five elephants.

More than a mall There's plenty to do other than just shop. The entrance and ticket office to the two viewing platforms in Burj Khalifa (▷ 62–63) is on the lower ground floors and Dubai Aquarium (▷ opposite) is built into the fabric of the mall. Young visitors will love KidZania (▷ 77), Sega Republic (▷ 73) and the ice-skating rink, and entertainment for the whole family is on-screen at the cinema complex. There are plenty of places to eat, from fine dining to snacks, including a selection set along the waterfront promenade with views of Burj Khalifa and overlooking the lake for front-row seats for The Dubai Fountain show (▷ 66–67).

THE BASICS

www.thedubaimall.com
🗺 B6
✉ Financial Center Road, off Sheikh Zayed Road
☎ 800 38244 6255 (800 Dubai-Mall)
🕐 Sun–Wed 10am–midnight, Thu–Sat 10am–1am
🍴 Many options
🚇 Burj Khalifa/Dubai Mall
♿ Excellent

HIGHLIGHTS

● The combination of activities
● Fashion Avenue for the concentration of big names
● The lakefront promenade with views of Burj Khalifa and The Dubai Fountain
● Over 80 child-centric role-play activities at KidZania

TIP

● The mall rents out lockers so you don't have to carry your purchases around.

The Dubai Fountain

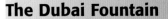

TOP 25

The world's largest dancing fountain show has been wildly popular since it first broke water in 2009, and, to date, 47 million people have taken a lakeside seat for its shimmering, swaying performances.

Water The design has a 275m (900ft) long thread of jets, supplemented by five circles, just under 1,500 water jets in all, along with 1,000 fog jets. During the performance, 83,000 liters (22,000 gallons) of water becomes airborne, and the jets of water shoot 150m (500ft) into the air—the height of a 50-story building.

Music and lights But water is only part of the whole. Some 6,600 "superlights" and 25 color projectors create 1.5 million lumens of light for-mulated into over 1,000 abstract creations. The

View looking down from the Burj Khalifa; the dancing fountains at sunset; and at night (clockwise from left)

beams can be seen over 32km (20 miles) away. And of course there's the music. There's a varied repertoire, including the specially penned piece *Sama Dubai*. Others include the haunting *Time to Say Goodbye (Con te partiro)* sung by Andrea Bocelli, *Baba Yetu*, an award-winning song in Swahili, and a top-selling Arabic dance track, *Shik Shak Shok*. For the closest views of the evening dancing shows, take a trip onto the lake on an electrically powered *abra*. The ticket office is at the waterfront promenade of The Dubai Mall.

WET California-based WET is the world leader in this field. Creator of the fountains at the Bellagio and Mirage on the Vegas strip, WET designed the Olympic cauldron at Salt Lake City in 2002 and the fountains at the Olympic Park in Sochi in 2014.

THE BASICS

www.dubaimall.com

➕ A6

✉ Burj Khalifa Lake, Downtown Dubai

☎ Enquiries through The Dubai Mall 800 38244 6255 (800 Dubai-Mall)

🕐 Daily at 1, 1.30 and every 30 mins from 6pm–11pm

🚇 Burj Khalifa/Dubai Mall

♿ Very good

🎟 Free, *abra* ride moderate

Ras al Khor Wildlife Sanctuary

TOP 25

A rare and precious wetland at the head of the 14km (8.5-mile) long Dubai Creek, this tiny sanctuary, only 6.2 sq km (2.4 sq miles) in area, is vital for the 20,000 birds that spend their winters here.

Natural environment A *khor* is a shallow tidal inlet where sediment accumulates. Ras al Khor sits at the interface between the creek and the desert, comprising areas of intertidal mudflats, mangroves, reed beds, pools, and *sabkha* (salt-encrusted flats). The maximum depth of the water is 2m (6.5ft) with a tidal range of between 1m (3.2ft) and 1.5m (4.9ft). It's an environment that supports more than 500 species of flora and fauna—at the peak of the winter season, 67 different species settle here, including dunlins, godwits, curlews, redshanks, Little Stints and sandwich terns. There are

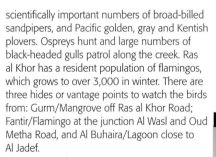

Pink flamingos feed at Ras al Khor Wildlife Sanctuary, with the towers of the city clearly visible in the distance

scientifically important numbers of broad-billed sandpipers, and Pacific golden, gray and Kentish plovers. Ospreys hunt and large numbers of black-headed gulls patrol along the creek. Ras al Khor has a resident population of flamingos, which grows to over 3,000 in winter. There are three hides or vantage points to watch the birds from: Gurm/Mangrove off Ras al Khor Road; Fantir/Flamingo at the junction Al Wasl and Oud Metha Road, and Al Buhaira/Lagoon close to Al Jadef.

The future Ras al Khor was the one area of Dubai that benefited from the global financial crisis, when several developments planned to abut the sanctuary were put on hold or cancelled completely. As the economy bounces back, conservationists will once again be keeping a watching brief on the creek head.

THE BASICS

www.wildlife.ae

➕ Off map at D9

✉ Off Ras al Khor Road

☎ 606 6822

🕐 Sat–Thu 9–4

♿ None

💵 Free

TIPS

● Binoculars will help you get the most out of your visit.

● There are no refreshment stands or machines, so take drinks and food with you.

● November to March is the best time of year to visit.

● Visit early or late in the day to watch the birds feeding.

More to See

AL QUOZ ART GALLERIES

www.alserkalavenue.ae

Lying equidistant between Burj Khalifa (▷ 62–63) and Mall of the Emirates (▷ 93), Al Quoz is a small district of low-rise commercial properties and warehouses that, over the last 20 years or so, has seen the impromptu rise of an urban arts center. It's somewhat of an anomaly in a city where just about every community is planned down to the last detail, but more than 20 galleries and organizations can be found around the nucleus of Alserkal Avenue.

➕ Off map at A5 ✉ 8th Street, Al Quoz District ☎ 416 1900 ♿ Few/good

DOWNTOWN DUBAI

www.mydowntowndubai.com

One of Sheikh Mohammed's pet projects, this vast planned community was designed to emulate the spirit of old Dubai, and develop Sheikh Zayed Road area beyond its role as a business and convention district. The community motto is "The Center of Now", which rings true—it acts as a magnet for visitors, with the flagship Burj Khalifa (▷ 62–63), The Dubai Fountain (▷ 66–67), The Dubai Mall (▷ 65), and Old Town (▷ 72–73) all sitting within its boundaries. There are several business and residential areas, plus Sheikh Mohammed bin Rashid Boulevard encircling the district, with its shopping and dining opportunities, street fairs and festivals.

➕ A6 ✉ Sheikh Mohammed bin Rashid Boulevard, off Financial Center Road ☎ Customer Center 367 3333 🚇 Burj Khalifa/Dubai Mall ♿ Excellent 🚌 Boulevard bus tour inexpensive

DUBAI WORLD TRADE CENTER

www.dwtc.com

See where Dubai's transformation from desert trading outpost to home of world-class skyscrapers really kicked off, at the city's first tower. The Dubai World Trade Center has a single, but significant, claim to fame. This honeycombed structure, 149m (488ft) tall, was

Dubai World Trade Center

Inside the Emirates Towers

Dubai's first skyscraper when it was completed in 1979. Since then, ever more elaborate skyscrapers have marched down Sheikh Zayed Road. It might look dated, but the World Trade Center tower was the precursor to modern Dubai.

➕ F5 ✉ Trade Center Roundabout ☎ 332 1000 🚇 World Trade Center ♿ Good

EMIRATES TOWERS

www.jumeirah.com

These futuristic twin towers were the first of Dubai's skyscrapers to test the boundaries of what could be created. The contrast with the Dubai World Trade Center couldn't be greater: The city's first skyscraper retains a certain 1970s charm, but the Emirates Towers' piercing apexes symbolized Dubai's drive to succeed. Designed by the Norr Group, the taller of the towers was completed in November 1999 at an official height of 354.6m (1,163ft). Its shorter partner (at 305m/1,000ft) was completed on April 15 2000. If seeing the view from the top isn't enough, there's a thoroughly masochistic way to see the Emirates Towers: a vertical marathon. Competitors—it's open to anyone—have to run up the 1,334 steps linking the 52 floors of the Jumeirah Emirates Towers hotel, a distance of 265 vertical metres (869ft).

➕ D5 ✉ Sheikh Zayed Road ☎ Hotel 330 0000 🍴 Restaurants and bars in the Jumeirah Emirates Towers hotel, and cafés in the Boulevard mall ♿ Excellent 🚇 Emirates Towers

GATE VILLAGE

www.difc.ae

Dubai International Financial Center is one of the city's major Free Zones, a planned community catering to the financial services sector. Characterized by a series of dull high-rise towers, the district is dominated by The Gate, a distinctive Gensier-designed 15-story glass-sided arch. Gate Village is the social hub of the financial district,

Emirates Towers

The Gate, Dubai International Finance Center

More to See

with a range of shopping and dining establishments. This is a burgeoning center for the arts, with over a dozen high-end galleries and regular arts-related events. Visit the Opera Gallery (www.operagallery. com), which displays works by Chagall, Miró, Picasso and Rodin.

✚ D5 ✉ 7th Street, off Sheikh Zayed Road ☎ International Financial Center admin: 362 2222 🚇 Emirates Towers ♿ Excellent

MEYDAN COMPLEX

www.meydan.ae
www.dubairacingclub.com

Race night at the stylish Meydan racecourse is an important social event in Dubai, and also an opportunity to see some of the finest Arabian horses in action, so it should be an essential part of any wintertime visit to Dubai. The track features a 2,400m (2,624yd) long turf course inside a 1,750m (1,913yd) all-weather course, running past the grandstand with its distinctive crescent-shaped roof. The illegality of gambling in the United Arab Emirates has been circumvented by the giving away of prizes for correct predictions of race results. The whole of Dubai society turns up for the World Cup races in March and, if you are lucky enough to find a space among the 60,000 spectators, it is a great opportunity for watching people as well as horses.

✚ Off map at B9 ✉ Off Al Ain–Dubai road; signposted from Interchange 1 and 2 of Sheikh Zayed Road ☎ 332 2277 🕐 Race nights: Oct–Apr Thu 7pm ♿ Excellent
🅿 General admission and parking free (except for Dubai World Cup race)

OLD TOWN

In the heart of high-rise Downtown Dubai (▷ 70) this tiny enclave is a low-rise homage to the traditional Arabic architecture found in old Al Bastakiya (▷ 24) and Shindagha (▷ 32–33) in Bur Dubai. Its alleyways and squares are sprinkled with cafés, and the traditionally styled Souk al Bahar sells a range of local arts and handicrafts. It's a great

Meydan racecourse

Horses and jockeys on the Meydan race track

place to explore while waiting for the next performance of The Dubai Fountain (▷ 66–67).

🔢 A6 ✉ Off Sheikh Mohammed bin Rashid Boulevard ☎ Customer Center: 367 3333 🚇 Burj Khalifa/Dubai Mall ♿ Excellent

SEGA REPUBLIC

www.segarepublic.com

The Japanese multinational SEGA is one of the world's leaders in electronic gaming. Founded as early as 1940 in Honolulu, Hawaii, as Service Games, the company moved to Tokyo in 1954 and began importing American arcade games. It soon moved into manufacturing under the name SEGA (taking the first two letters from SErvice GAmes) and entered the console market in the 1980s. Its Sonic the Hedgehog character, mascot of the company, was introduced in 1991. SEGA Republic is an indoor theme-park heaven covering 7,000 sq m (76,000 sq ft). The play area has 14 high-tech adrenalin-fuelled attractions and 170 SEGA games, and is specifically aimed at children—of all ages.

🔢 B7 ✉ The Dubai Mall ☎ 448 8484 🕐 Sun–Wed 10am–midnight, Thu–Sat 10am–1am 🚇 Burj Khalifa/Dubai Mall ♿ Very good 💵 Expensive

ZABEEL PARK

Take a break from shopping and sightseeing in the city center with a stroll around the first technology-themed park in the Middle East, providing a 47ha (116-acre) green respite from downtown Dubai. Stretching either side of the Sheikh Zayed Expressway, the two sections are linked by a bridge suspended from a 52m (170 ft) spar and 16 steel cables. There's plenty to do; the Stargate dome houses an IMAX screen, and the egg-shaped, 2,000-capacity Megabowl amphitheater hosts live music shows. Enjoy a boat trip on the lake or play mini-golf. You can tour the park on a mini-train or rent a Segway.

🔢 G6 ✉ Zabeel ☎ 398 6888 🕐 Daily 8am–11pm ♿ Good 💵 Inexpensive

The entrance to SEGA Republic, inside The Dubai Mall

Palm trees in Zabeel Park

Shopping

NORTH SHEIKH ZAYED ROAD AND ZABEEL MALLS

This area is home to the big one, The Dubai Mall (▷ 65, www.the dubaimall.com), but there are other quality shopping districts if you'd prefer something smaller and more personal. Souk Al Bahar (www.soukalbahar. ae) in Downtown Dubai offers excellent choice in handicrafts. In the south of the district, the Gold and Diamond Park (www. goldanddiamondpark. com) is the modern air-conditioned equivalent of the Gold Souk in Deira—though it lacks the atmosphere. Nearby Al Quoz has a good range of art galleries.

ABDUL SAMAD AL QURASHI

www.thedubaimall.com
Selling a range of traditional *ittars*, Oudh and incenses, this is an excellent location to research some of the rich scents that make up an Arabian fragrance.

➕ B6 ✉ The Dubai Mall ☎ 388 2780 🕐 Sun–Wed 10am–midnight, Thu–Sat 10am–1am 🚇 Burj Khalifa/Dubai Mall

AL SHAREIF GALLERY

www.pch.ae
Handicrafts imported from around the Gulf including ceramics, inlaid wooden boxes and backgammon sets, and gilded metalware.

➕ B6 ✉ The Souk, The Dubai Mall ☎ 388 2211 🕐 Sun–Wed 10am–midnight, Thu–Sat 10am–1am 🚇 Burj Khalifa/Dubai Mall

THE AQUARIUM STORE

www.thedubaimall.com
Gift shop of the Dubai Aquarium & Underwater Zoo, but you don't need to buy a ticket to shop here. There's something for every budget from keyrings to one-of-a-kind artworks.

➕ B6 ✉ The Dubai Mall ☎ 325 3337 🕐 Sun–Wed 10am–midnight, Thu–Sat 10am–1am 🚇 Burj Khalifa/ Dubai Mall

ARABIAN TREASURES

www.thedubaimall.com
Small boutique selling

GALLERY ONE

When Gregg and Jane Sedgwick opened their first Gallery One shop in 2005 they had one clear aim—to "democratize" art. They felt that many prospective buyers were intimidated by the gallery "experience" of empty rooms where fellow browsers are few and conversations are held in whispers, so they set out to make the Gallery One experience warm and friendly, and they seem to be succeeding. They now have ten stores across the Persian Gulf and are still growing.

---

unusual antique Arabian jewelry, silver, metal handicrafts, and delicate prayer beads in semi-precious stones such as agate and amber.

➕ B6 ✉ The Souk, The Dubai Mall ☎ 325 3337 🕐 Sun–Wed 10am–midnight, Thu–Sat 10am–1am 🚇 Burj Khalifa/Dubai Mall

THE CAMEL COMPANY

www.camelcompany.ae
Everyone loves a camel, so why not stock up on camel-related souvenirs? Mugs, T-shirts and ceramics match cuddly camels of every size.

➕ A6 ✉ Souk al Bahar, Old Town ☎ 388 4559 🕐 Sat–Thu 10–10, Fri 2–10 🚇 Burj Khalifa/Dubai Mall

CEYLON MASTER GEMS

www.ceylonmastergems.com
This small jewelers specializes in high-quality colored stones. Come here for sapphires, rubies and emeralds, loose or set in finished pieces.

➕ e1 ✉ Gold and Diamond Park, Interchange 4, Sheikh Zayed Road, Al Quoz (3) ☎ 340 4310 🕐 Sat–Thu 10–10, Fri 4–10

CHETAN

www.goldanddiamondpark.com
Chetan has an excellent range of diamond and gem jewelry with many sets of diamond earrings and necklaces.

➕ e1 ✉ Gold and

Diamond Park, Interchange 4, Sheikh Zayed Road, Al Quoz (3) ☎ 340 4644 🕐 Sat–Thu 10–10, Fri 4–10

THE COBBLER
www.thecobbler.ae
An old-fashioned gentleman's emporium selling bespoke leather shoes, and providing high-quality accessories including socks, polishes and brushes. Another branch can be found in The Dubai Mall.
➕ D5 ✉ Dubai International Financial Center ☎ 386 3490 🕐 Sun–Thu 9–7, Sat 9–6. Closed Fri 🚇 Financial Center

CUADRO
www.caudroart.com
A fine art gallery for the discerning collector with pieces in all genres, plus knowledgeable staff to advise prospective buyers.
➕ D5 ✉ Gate Village, Dubai International Financial Center ☎ 425 0400 🕐 Sun–Thu 10–8, Sat noon–6. Closed Fri 🚇 Financial Center

DAMAS
www.damasjewellery.com
Internationally renowned jewelers with outlets in 18 countries, Damas stock ranges by the finest manufacturers including Tiffany & Co and Gucci.
➕ B6 ✉ The Souk, The Dubai Mall ☎ 339 8846 🕐 Sun–Wed 10am–midnight, Thu–Sat 10am–1am 🚇 Burj Khalifa/Dubai Mall

THE EMPTY QUARTER FINE ART PHOTOGRAPHY
www.theemptyquarter.com
Currently the only gallery in Dubai dealing exclusively in photographic images. There's an impressive collection from around the world, but it's the local images that may be the more appealing.
➕ D5 ✉ Gate Village, Dubai International Financial Center ☎ 323 1210 🕐 Sat–Thu 10–8. Closed Fri 🚇 Financial Center

GALLERY ONE
www.g-1.com
The best place for affordable prints and art relating to Dubai—these may not be one-of-a-kind, but they certainly have some evocative images that make great souvenirs.

LITTLE GEMS
When buying gemstones, the price depends on four factors:
● Cut: Is it a good shape? Does it reflect light well?
● Clarity: Are there any inclusions (foreign bodies) in the stone and, if so, how big?
● Color: All gemstones have an ideal color.
● Carat weight: Stones are weighed in carats (each carat is 0.2 grams). Generally, the more a stone weighs the bigger it is.

➕ A6 ✉ Souk al Bahar, Old Town ☎ 420 3619 🕐 Sat–Thu 10–10, Fri 2–10 🚇 Burj Khalifa/Dubai Mall

THE HANDICRAFT GALLERY
www.thehandicraftgallery.com
High-quality clothing and handicrafts imported from Kashmir in northern India. Carved jewelry boxes, papier-mâché decorations, silk pashminas and hand-stitched rugs are among the range on sale.
➕ Off map ✉ Oasis Center, off Sheikh Zayed Road, Al Quoz (3) ☎ 050 887 4962 🕐 Sun–Thu 10–10, Thu–Sat 10am–midnight

MIRI CREATION
www.miricreation.ae
A small but quality collection of handmade Persian rugs and carpets hand-woven from wool colored with natural dyes. Also ceramics and decorative items.
➕ B6 ✉ The Dubai Mall ☎ 434 0433 🕐 Sun–Wed 10am–midnight, Thu–Sat 10am–1am 🚇 Burj Khalifa/Dubai Mall

MOMENTUM
www.momentum-dubai.com
An impressive collection of vintage and antique timepieces, including very rare and valuable specimens.
➕ D5 ✉ Dubai International Financial Center ☎ 327 4320 🕐 Sun–Thu 10–8, Sat noon–6. Closed Fri 🚇 Financial Center

Entertainment and Nightlife

ARMANI/PRIVÉ

www.armanihotels.com

One of Dubai's coolest clubs in the ultra-chic Armani Hotel, Burj Khalifa, Privé plays to a refined clientele. Dress accordingly.
✚ B6 ✉ Armani Hotel, Burj Khalifa ☎ 888 3888 🕐 Mon–Sat 10pm–3am 🚇 Burj Khalifa/Dubai Mall

BLUE BAR

www.novotel.com

This long-standing Dubai venue has live blues at weekends and a recorded repertoire on weekdays. It's a rare chance to get a genuine blues vibe in the city.
✚ E5 ✉ Novotel, Zabeel Road 2, off Sheikh Zayed Road, Trade Center (1) ☎ 332 0000 🕐 Daily 2–2 🚇 World Trade Center

CALABAR

www.theaddress.com

The expansive outside terrace is the draw at Calabar. Enjoy a cool drink under the palms with the lights of Downtown Dubai twinkling all around, and you'll have a ringside seat for The Dubai Fountain (▷ 66–67).
✚ A6 ✉ The Address, Downtown Dubai ☎ 888 3444 🕐 Daily 6pm–2.30am 🚇 Burj Khalifa/Dubai Mall

THE EMIRATES A380 EXPERIENCE

www.emirates380experience.com

This genuine flight simulator allows you to get behind the controls of an Emirates Airlines A380. Choose one of 12 locations to make your landing and go for it.
✚ B6 ✉ The Dubai Mall ☎ 388 2915 🕐 Showings noon–midnight 🚇 Burj Khalifa/Dubai Mall

FEET LOUNGE

www.feetlounge.ae

Offering Thai massage and reflexology sessions (massage specifically for the feet), this small spa makes a great place to restore energy to the toes that walk the malls and museums all day.
✚ Off map ✉ Executive Towers, Bay Avenue, Business Bay ☎ 452 2259 🕐 Sun–Thu noon–10, Fri–Sat 10–10 🚇 Business Bay

FLEURS

www.fleursclub.com

An intimate weekend-only venue with a range of live performances, audiences are encouraged to throw flowers at the performers to show their appreciation, hence the name—Fleurs is French for "flowers".
✚ E5 ✉ Radisson Royal Hotel, Sheikh Zayed Road, Trade Center (1) ☎ 050 913 9148 🕐 Thu–Fri 9pm–2am 🚇 World Trade Center

THE FRIDGE

www.thefridgedubai.com

One of the leading arts organizations in Dubai, operating a fluid structure that supports concerts and exhibitions both at their HQ in Al Quoz and at venues around the city.
✚ Off map ✉ Off Alserkal Avenue, Al Quoz (1) ☎ 347 7793 🕐 Varied calendar

THE GALLERY AT EMAAR PAVILION

www.emaargallery.com

Dubai property giants Emaar have funded Dubai's most exciting new art space in the heart of their Downtown Dubai development. The gallery will feature a program of exhibitions by established and emerging international and local artists.
✚ A6 ✉ Mohammed Bin Rashid Boulevard, Downtown Dubai ☎ 428 7938 🕐 Sat–Thu 9–6 🚇 Burj Khalifa/Dubai Mall

HARRY GHATTO'S

www.jumeirah.com

The best karaoke bar in Dubai starts late and you

THE ARTS

The arts scene is growing and is set for a big boost. It's already a regional hub for the classics, with a small season of concerts and exhibitions, and a handful of quality galleries showcasing Middle Eastern and international artists. The building of the Dubai Modern Art Museum and Opera House, a 2,000 seat multi-function auditorium close to Burj Khalifa due to be inaugurated in 2015, will cement this position still further.

can continue crooning until 3am. It's a compact place, behind the Tokyo restaurant, but that just adds to the atmosphere. ✚ D5 ✉ The Boulevard, Jumeirah Emirates Towers ☎ 330 0000 🕐 Daily 12pm–3am (Fri 4pm–3am), karaoke from 10pm (Fri 5pm) Ⓜ Emirates Towers

IKANDY

www.shangri-la.com
The Shangri-La pool deck is transformed as the sun goes down into one of the coolest clubs in the city. The clientele is uber-fashionable and the views are spectacular. ✚ C5 ✉ Shangri-La, Sheikh Zayed Road ☎ 343 8888 🕐 Daily 6pm–2am Ⓜ Financial Center

THE IVY JAZZ LOUNGE

www.theivy.ae
The Ivy has filled a gap in the market with its range of live jazz, from trad to swing, working closely with talent at The Fridge (▷ 76) to create a varied program of sessions. ✚ D5 ✉ The Boulevard, Jumeirah Emirates Towers ☎ 319 8767 🕐 Lounge daily noon–2am, live music Tue and Thu 9pm, Fri 11am–2am Ⓜ Emirates Towers

KIDZANIA

www.kidzania.ae
When kids want to play adult for the day, bring them to KidZania. This supervised role-play attraction allows them to choose from 80 activities,

including fire fighter, doctor or TV presenter, and the realistic stage sets mean they get to operate in the KidZania real world. ✚ B6 ✉ The Dubai Mall ☎ 448 5222 🕐 Sun–Wed 9am–11pm, Thu 9am–midnight, Fri–Sat 10am–midnight Ⓜ Burj Khalifa/Dubai Mall

LEVEL 43 SKY LOUNGE

www.level43lounge.com
Open throughout the day, this rooftop lounge on the 43rd floor really comes to life in the evenings when the lights of Sheikh Zayed Road and Burj Khalifa look amazing. ✚ D5 ✉ Four Points by Sheraton Sheikh Zayed Road, Trade Center (1) ☎ 323 0333 🕐 Daily 11am–2am Ⓜ Financial Center

REEL CINEMAS

www.reelcinemas.ae
With 22 screens, this is the flagship complex of Reel Cinemas. The

---

FILMS

It takes a while for Hollywood's latest hit films to filter through to Dubai's cinemas. Every film has to be assessed by the emirate's film censors, who take a hardline attitude to any controversial themes or subject matter—typically this includes political or sexual content. Films that are released in Dubai may also be edited for language and other content.

Picturehouse theater is dedicated to art movies, there are 3D theaters, and there are extra-comfortable leather lounge seats in the Platinum Movie Suites. ✚ B6 ✉ The Dubai Mall ☎ 449 1988 🕐 Showings noon–midnight Ⓜ Burj Khalifa/Dubai Mall

THE THIRD EYE

www.thethirdeye.com
A mind and body center which brings together practitioners from many wellbeing and new age therapies. Visit here for reiki energy sessions, chakra awakening and angel readings. ✚ C5 ✉ 1101 Saeed Tower, Sheikh Zayed Road, Trade Center (2) ☎ 326 6539 🕐 Calendar of sessions throughout the week Ⓜ Emirates Towers

THE STABLES

Lively sports bar with English menu and live soccer on the one hand, and bucking bronco and live bands in the Rodeo Drive section. It attracts a down-to-earth crowd. ✚ E5 ✉ Next to the Radisson Royal Hotel, Sheikh Zayed Road, Trade Center (1) ☎ 05 2814 1127 🕐 Daily 6pm–2am Ⓜ Trade Center

TRADER VIC'S

www.tradervics.com
The cocktails are the chief attraction at this long-standing Polynesian-themed bar/restaurant, and it remains popular as

a place to get a cheap and cheerful evening drink. Two other locations in the city: Festival City and Madinat Jumeirah.

➕ D–E5 ✉ Crowne Plaza Hotel, Sheikh Zayed Road ☎ 311 1111 🕐 Sat–Thu 6.30pm–1.30am, Fri 7.30pm–11.30pm 🚇 Emirates Towers

WHITE

www.whitedubai.com

A massive open-air night-club that broke on to the scene in 2013 and immediately became a hit. The experience is "big" in so many ways,

with thousands of people enjoying the energy.

➕ Off map at B9 ✉ Meydan Racecourse ☎ 50 433 0933 🕐 End Sep–late Jun

VU'S

www.jumeirah.com

Take the high-speed lift to the 51st floor of the Jumeirah Emirates Towers for one of the headiest views in town: Few places look as futuristic as Sheikh Zayed Road at night. This is a must-visit bar, although the cocktail prices may bring you back to earth.

➕ D5 ✉ Jumeirah Emirates Towers Hotel ☎ 330 0000 🕐 Daily 5pm–2am 🚇 Emirates Towers

ZINC

www.ihg.com

Zinc is a popular night-club aimed at people who want to party rather than strike a pose. The music is determinedly mainstream and "happy hour" drinks deals are generous.

➕ D–E5 ✉ Crowne Plaza Hotel, Sheikh Zayed Road ☎ 331 1111 🕐 Daily 7pm–3am 🚇 Emirates Towers

Restaurants

PRICES

Prices are approximate, based on a 3-course meal for one person.
$$$ over 300 AED
$$ 150-300 AED
$ under 150 AED

ABDEL WAHAB ($$–$$$)

www.soukalbahar.ae

The contemporary decor is at odds with the traditional Lebanese menu but grab a table on the terrace for great views of The Dubai Fountain as you eat.

➕ A6 ✉ Souk al Bahar, Old Town ☎ 423 0988 🕐 Lunch, dinner 🚇 Burj Khalifa/Dubai Mall

AL MANDALOUN ($–$$)

www.al-mandaloun.com

For a taste of delicious Lebanese food, try this superb contemporary

THE IVY

Dubai's The Ivy is the young sibling of one of London's top addresses. An unassuming eatery in the heart of theaterland, it opened in 1916 as a simple Italian café, and soon attracted tired thespians needing to recharge after a performance. Now everyone from Nicole Kidman to the Beckhams calls in when they're in town.

restaurant. The cooking covers all bases, including fattoush, kebabs, and stuffed vine leaves.

➕ D5 ✉ Dubai International Financial Center ☎ 363 7474 🕐 Breakfast, lunch, dinner. Closed Sun 🚇 Financial Center

AMAL ($$$)

www.armanihotels.com

This upscale Indian restaurant is currently one of the go-to places in the emirate. The dishes are exquisitely spiced and the interior decor correspondingly "cool".

➕ B6 ✉ Armani Hotel, Burj Khalifa ☎ 888 3888 🕐 Dinner 🚇 Burj Khalifa/Dubai Mall

CAFÉ HABANA ($$)

www.soukalbahar.ae

Great cocktails and Mexican/Latin food in a bar styled like a slice of Hemingway's Havana.

🏠 A6 ✉ Souk al Bahar, Old Town ☎ 422 2620 ⏰ Lunch, dinner 🚇 Burj Khalifa/Dubai Mall

CARLUCCIO'S ($–$$)

www.carluccios.com

Antonio Carluccio brings his relaxed Italian staples to Dubai, with a range of pizzas, pastas and excellent antipasti. This is celebrity chef dining without the ritzy price tag.

🏠 B6 ✉ The Dubai Mall ☎ 434 1320 ⏰ Lunch, dinner 🚇 Burj Khalifa/Dubai Mall

CLAW BBQ ($$)

www.soukalbahar.ae

Comfort food, southern style, in the heart of Downtown Dubai. Claw supplies starters like peel-n-eat shrimp with buckets of crab claws to follow. Bibs are supplied, just like back in Louisiana.

🏠 A6 ✉ Souk al Bahar, Old Town ☎ 423 2300 ⏰ Lunch, dinner 🚇 Burj Khalifa/Dubai Mall

CUT ($$$)

www.wolfgangpuck.com

With a modern steak menu by celebrity chef Wolfgang Puck, Cut is big news. Aged Wagyu, Australian Angus and Prime US beef can be combined with a range of fusion sauces and sides.

There's a fixed-price two-course lunch.

🏠 A6 ✉ The Address, Downtown Dubai ☎ 888 3444 ⏰ Lunch, dinner. Closed Sat lunch 🚇 Burj Khalifa/Dubai Mall

EXCHANGE GRILL ($$$)

www.fairmont.com

The Exchange Grill's dining room can seem austere by Dubai standards but superb steaks and an outstanding wine list create a warm glow. Meat lovers can't help but be satisfied.

🏠 E5 ✉ Fairmont Hotel, Sheikh Zayed Road ☎ 311 8316 ⏰ Dinner 🚇 World Trade Center

LA FARINE CAFÉ AND BAKERY ($–$$)

www.marriott.com

Open 24 hours a day for coffee and pastries, La Farine is great to visit after

---

BUDDHA AND KARMA

Karma Kafé is the latest concept by innovative trendsetter Raymond Visan. He kick-started a modern phenomenon when he opened his first Buddha Bar in Paris in 1996 along with designer Claude Challe. This revolutionary casual eatery/lounge captured the dinner crowd, who then stayed on into the early hours, listening to resident DJs turning a mix of chill-out music. It's a concept that's now gone worldwide.

---

a night on the town. It also offers one of the best afternoon teas in Dubai.

🏠 Off map ✉ JW Marriott Marquis, Business Bay ☎ 414 3000 ⏰ Breakfast, lunch, dinner (24 hours) 🚇 Business Bay

HOI AN ($$$)

www.shangri-la.com

In a convincing mock-Saigon-style dining room, silk-clad waitresses serve delicious Vietnamese dishes. Starters include Saigon street-vendor soup, a clear broth with translucent noodles, chicken and black mushrooms. For the main course, clay-pot chicken is a tasty, tangy choice. Hoi-An is a treat.

🏠 C5 ✉ Shangri-La, Sheikh Zayed Road ☎ 405 2703 ⏰ Dinner 🚇 Financial Center

THE IVY ($$$)

www.theivy.ae

This classic London theaterland favorite has now arrived in Dubai offering its signature shepherd's pie and sticky toffee pudding—plus other British classics—in much better weather.

🏠 D5 ✉ The Boulevard, Jumeirah Emirates Towers ☎ 319 8767 ⏰ Breakfast, lunch, dinner 🚇 Emirates Towers

KARMA KAFÉ ($$)

www.karma-kafe.com

This cool restaurant, bar and lounge has been a big hit for its Asian

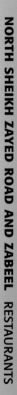

menu—inspired by Japan, China and Thailand among others. Come for dinner and stay late for drinks.

✚ A6 ✉ Souk al Bahar, Old Town ☎ 423 0909 🕐 Dinner, lunch Fri, Sat 🚇 Burj Khalifa/Dubai Mall

THE NOODLE HOUSE ($)

www.thenoodlehouse.com
Several outlets of this chain exist around Dubai. They serve up a choice of tasty and inexpensive noodle and rice dishes, plus other pan-Asian standbys. A good option for a quick, low-cost lunch or dinner.

✚ D5 ✉ The Boulevard, Jumeirah Emirates Towers ☎ 319 8088 🕐 Lunch, dinner 🚇 Emirates Towers

ORIGINAL WINGS AND RINGS ($–$$)

www.buffalo-arabia.com
Heaps of freshly cooked American bar food—so great chicken wings and onion rings, burgers and fries. A lively sports bar with big screens.

✚ C5 ✉ Liberty House, Sheikh Zayed Road, Trade Center (2) ☎ 359 6900 🕐 Lunch, dinner 🚇 Financial Center

THE RIB ROOM ($$–$$$)

www.jumeirah.com
Top-flight meat served to appreciative and loyal clients. The minimalist decor allows you to concentrate on the food. The Saturday brunch features live jazz music.

✚ D5 ✉ Jumeirah Emirates Towers ☎ 319 8088 🕐 Lunch, dinner. Closed Fri, Sat 🚇 Financial Center

TAQADO MEXICAN KITCHEN ($)

A tasty, simple mid-shopping option. Choose your meat, choose your filling, toppings plus a side order and there you have it. From burritos to tacos, there are no surprises.

✚ D5 ✉ Gate Building 5, Dubai International Financial Center ☎ 351 5210 🕐 Breakfast, lunch, dinner 🚇 Financial Center

UMAI ($$$)

www.oberoihotels.com
Umai allows you a tour around the cuisines of Asia with an open-kitchen concept of several different cooking stations. The decor and ambience are upscale.

✚ Off map ✉ The Oberoi, Business Bay ☎ 444 1407 🕐 Lunch, dinner. Closed Fri lunch and Sat 🚇 Business Bay

WHEELER'S OF ST JAMES ($$$)

www.wheelersdubai.com
Marco Pierre White brings his inimitable style to Dubai, with classy British dishes. Fish is a specialty and the chilled seafood platter is the signature dish.

✚ D5 ✉ Gate Village, Dubai International Financial Center ☎ 386 0899 🕐 Lunch, dinner 🚇 Finance Center or Emirates Towers

ZAATAR W ZEIT ($)

www.dubaimall.com
For a snack, light lunch or late supper during a shopping spree, enjoy a tasty budget *shwarma* from this small modern café.

✚ B6 ✉ The Dubai Mall ☎ 435 8310 🕐 Lunch, dinner 🚇 Burj Khalifa/Dubai Mall

ZAROOB ($–$$)

www.zaroob.com
If you'd like to try Lebanese cuisine but don't want a budget street café then Zaroob could fit the bill. The decor has an urban-café feel and the menu is right on the button.

✚ D5 ✉ Jumeirah Emirates Towers ☎ 327 6060 🕐 Breakfast, lunch, dinner (24 hours) 🚇 Emirates Towers

---

MARCO PIERRE WHITE

Brit Marco Pierre White is the self-styled *enfant terrible* of the chef-ing world. The youngest 3-star Michelin chef in history—achieved when he was only 33—White left school without any qualifications. He commenced training with Albert and Michel Roux at the renowned La Gavroche restaurant in London. In 1987 he opened his first restaurant, Harvey's, and won his first Michelin star in 1988.

Dubai's coastline has been transformed beyond recognition in the last 15 years in ways that push the boundaries of engineering expertise. From the dazzling new Dubai Marina, with its forest of high-rise towers, to the first of Dubai's mega-artificial islands, Palm Jumeirah, it plays host to a plethora of luxury beach resorts.

Sights	84–94	Top 25	TOP 25
Shopping	95	Atlantis, The Palm ▷ 84	
		Burj Al Arab ▷ 86	
Entertainment		Madinat Jumeirah ▷ 87	
and Nightlife	96–97	Jumeirah Mosque ▷ 88	
		Ski Dubai ▷ 90	
Restaurants	97–98	Wild Wadi ▷ 91	

Jumeirah and Dubai Marina

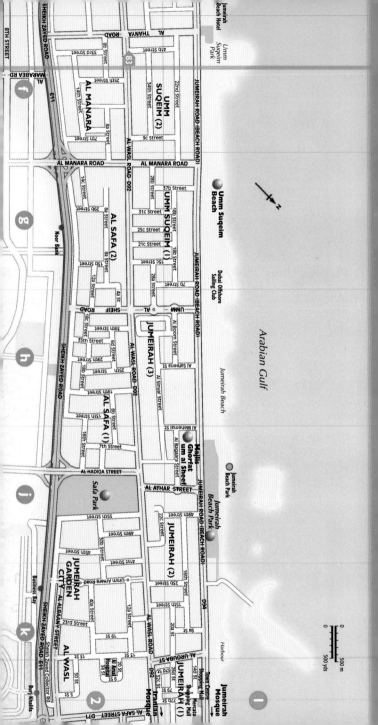

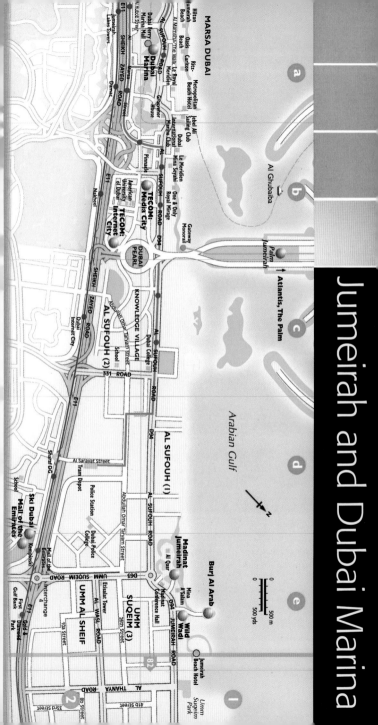

Jumeirah and Dubai Marina

MARSA DUBAI

Hilton Jumeirah Beach
Al Jumeirah Beach
Dubai Ferry
Marina Mall
Oasis Beach
Ritz-Carlton
Metropolitan Beach Hotel
Al Mamzar/The Walk / JBR
Al SUFOUH ROAD
Dubai Marina
Le Royal Meridien
Grosvenor House
Jebel Ali Sailing Club
Marina Walk
Pinnacle
Marina
Greens
Dubai International Marine Club
Le Meridien Mina Seyahi
One & Only Royal Mirage
E11
SHEIKH ZAYED ROAD
Damac
Nakheel
American University of Dubai
TECOM: Media City
Al SUFOUH ROAD
TECOM: Internet City
Gateway Monorail
DUBAI PEARL
Atlantis, The Palm
Palm Jumeirah
Al Ghubaiba
KNOWLEDGE VILLAGE
Al SUFOUH (2)
Dubai College
Sheikh Omar Tarjim Street
School
AL SUFOUH ROAD
331 ROAD
Dubai Internet City
SHEIKH ZAYED ROAD
E11
AL SUFOUH (1)
Arabian Gulf
Al Sarayat Street
Al Tram Depot
Police Station
Dubai Police College
Abdullah Omar Tarjim Street
AL SUFOUH ROAD
D94
N
Madinat Jumeirah
Al Qasr
Mina A'Salam
Madinat Conference Hall
Burj Al Arab
Wild Wadi
Sharaf DG
Ski Dubai / Mall of the Emirates
Kempinski
School
Interchange 4
UMM SUQEIM ROAD
First Gulf Bank
Gold & Diamond Park
E11
Mall of the Emirates
UMM AL SHEIF
Etisalat Tower
AL WASL ROAD
UMM SUQEIM (3)
26th Street
JUMEIRAH ROAD
D94
Jumeirah Beach Hotel
Umm Suqeim Park
82
AL THANYA ROAD
10a Street
33rd Street
80 Street
41b Street
2
D63

0   500 m
0   500 yds

E11

Atlantis, The Palm

Dubai's mega-resort is a veritable city within a city. Erupting out of the furthest point of The Palm like a pink wedding cake, the iconic structure is a pleasure dome for vacationers.

The hotel This is the biggest by far in Dubai. It has more than 1,500 rooms, with over 20 places to eat and several bars, lounges and nightclubs, all set on 1.4km (0.8 miles) of golden beach.

Aquaventure Waterpark There's excitement here for every age group. The Tower of Neptune area features a nine-story-high slide, and a tube slide through shark-infested waters. The Tower of Poseidon area, meanwhile, plays host to the world's largest waterslide, the UAE's only dual racing loop ride, and the longest zip-line ride in

Aquaventure Waterpark; the Lost Chambers Aquarium; meeting a dolphin at Dolphin Bay, in front of Atlantis, The Palm; a waterslide at Aquaventure Waterpark (clockwise from left)

the Middle East. Kids have their own specially designed area, Splashers, or they can make sand castles on Aquaventure Waterpark's private beach.

Dolphin Bay Several different "interactive" experiences are on offer, either in shallow or deeper water. The Dolphin Encounter is perfect for non-swimmers, while the Royal Swim is the ultimate package. At Sea Lion Point you can also take part in Sea Lion Discover interactive sessions, or drop by for a "kiss and cuddle" photo-op.

The Lost Chambers Aquarium Enter into a world inspired by the myth of the lost under-water city of Atlantis, where the ruins of old mansions and palaces house 20 tanks of different marine environments, home to more than 65,000 fish and marine creatures.

THE BASICS

www.atlantisthepalm.com
🔷 Off map at c1
✉ Crescent Road, The Palm
☎ Hotel reservations
426 2000
🕐 Open daily.
Aquaventure Waterpark:
daily 10am–sunset; The
Lost Chambers Aquarium:
daily 10am–midnight;
Dolphin Bay and Sealion
Point: daily—sessions must
be pre-booked.
🚉 Palm monorail
♿ Very good
💲 Activities expensive

85

Burj Al Arab

Views of the Burj Al Arab

THE BASICS

www.burj-al-arab.com

🔢 e1

✉ Beach Road, Jumeirah

☎ 301 7777

♿ Excellent

🍽 Expensive (minimum spend per person at the bar)

🚌 Jumeirah Beach Hotel

DID YOU KNOW?

The helipad atop the Burj Al Arab has been the venue of various sporting PR opportunities. In 2004, Tiger Woods teed off; in 2005, Federer and Agassi served and volleyed; in 2011 Rory McIlroy chipped out of a specially prepared bunker for a hole-in-one; and in 2013, David Coulthard burned rubber with some power donuts F1-style in a Red Bull speed machine.

One of the world's most recognizable contemporary buildings, Burj Al Arab broke the mold and—as the world's first seven-star hotel—redefined the luxury hospitality business. It also launched Dubai as a first-class tourist destination.

Inspiration It's fitting that Dubai's iconic building isn't a government edifice, a historic landmark or a place of worship. Architect Thomas Wills Wright was briefed to create something that would signal Dubai's ambitions to the world, but there are also references to Dubai's seafaring past in the sail-like facade made of a Teflon-coated, woven glass-fiber material. Inside it's a riot of color and, if it looks like gold, it probably is: 1,600sq m (17,000sqft) of gold leaf was used. The hotel's other vital statistics are equally jaw-dropping: there are 1,500 members of staff for 202 suites, each of which has its own butler. A fleet of 10 white Rolls-Royces is at the disposal of guests, while a helicopter shuttle service from the airport costs 10,000 AED.

Visiting The Burj Al Arab stands on its own man-made island 280m (918ft) offshore; if you're not staying here you'll need a reservation at one of the hotel's restaurants or bars to get inside. Admire the view along the coast from the Skyview Bar over a cocktail (though there's a minimum spend per person). Just as satisfying is to admire its grace and elegance from the outside, especially after dark when a light show plays across its surface.

TOP 25

Madinat Jumeirah

Madinat Jumeirah was Dubai's first planned tourism complex. A theme-park-style homage to Arabic architecture that some may find kitsch—think "One Thousand and One Nights"—it buzzes with energy.

What's here With three boutique hotels, 40 restaurants, a handful of entertainment venues and a shopping mall, Madinat Jumeirah is a self-contained resort. Among the towering *barjeels*, 4km (2.5 miles) of waterways, complete with motorized *abras* (extra cost) and a specially created shipwreck snake around the property, and lush greenery completes the oasis effect.

Souk Madinat It's air-conditioned and the prices are fixed, but this is a film-set fantasy of what a genuine souk could have looked like. With only 70 shops it is compact when compared to others in Dubai. There's a leaning towards quality regional crafts here, so the shops have more carpets, Arabic antiques and arts than fashion labels—in keeping with the theme.

After dark Madinat Theatre is one of only two in Dubai. It's an intimate 442-seat space with a varied program. Outside, live-music events are staged in the 1,000-seat amphitheater Madinat Arena, which backs onto a waterway. Pacha nightclub is on a similarly super-sized scale; the venue is one of the leading nights out for Dubai's party set, and many warm up beforehand in one of Madinat Jumeirah's excellent bars and restaurants.

THE BASICS

www.madinatjumeirah.com
🚻 e1
✉ Beach Road, at Umm Suqueim Road
☎ 366 8888
🍽 Many good cafés, restaurants and bars
♿ Good
🚤 Jumeirah Beach Hotel

HIGHLIGHTS

- The range of fashionable restaurants and bars
- Great nightlife
- The handicrafts in the stylized souk
- *Abra* rides along the canals

JUMEIRAH AND DUBAI MARINA TOP 25

Jumeirah Mosque

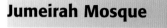

DID YOU KNOW?

If you miss seeing Jumeirah Mosque on your trip, you'll find an image of it on the 500 AED bank note.

DRESS CODE

Male and female visitors are expected to dress conservatively, covering arms and legs, and women should also wear a headscarf.

Jumeirah Mosque is the largest and most graceful mosque in the city, and it's the only one in Dubai regularly open to non-Muslims, offering visitors the chance to explore Islamic faith and architecture.

The architecture The mosque was built in 1975 in the medieval Fatimid style—the first flowering of Islamic architecture during the 9th–11th centuries—and is inspired by a larger mosque in Cairo, Egypt. The facade of the mosque has filigree stonework intended to add depth and warmth to the exterior. Inside, the deliberately low-key decoration has Turkish and Egyptian influences. A square arrangement of pillars supports the *qubba*, a central, painted dome, while the imam, or leader, faces Mecca from the *mehrab*, his pulpit.

The elegant Jumeirah Mosque, with its domed roofs and two minarets, is stunning both inside and out

Etiquette for worshipers Shoes are removed before entering the mosque as a sign of respect for other worshipers as Muslims pray and prostrate themselves on the floor. There is no physical distance between worshipers because everyone is equal: the sheikh prays alongside the taxi driver. A separate wing, behind the wooden doors to the left, is the women's prayer section—women don't worship with men in the United Arab Emirates. Joining the hour-long morning tour with a guide from the Sheikh Mohammed Center for Cultural Understanding (▷ 30) gives you a chance to admire not just the interior of the mosque, but also to find out anything you've ever wanted to know about Islam but didn't know how to ask—questions are encouraged. This is not a platform for proselytizing and the whole encounter is gently informative.

THE BASICS

✚ E2
✉ Beach Road
☎ 353 6666
🕐 Tours for non-Muslims at 10am (though it's advisable to get there early) on Sat–Thu with a guide from the Sheikh Mohammed Center for Cultural Understanding (▷ 30)
♿ Few
💰 Inexpensive
🏖 Jumeirah Open Beach

Ski Dubai

You can ski (left and right) or go tobogganing (center) among other attractions at Ski Dubai

THE BASICS

www.theplaymania.com/
skidubai

✚ d2

✉ Mall of the Emirates,
Interchange 4, Sheikh
Zayed Road

☎ 409 4090

🕐 Sat–Tue 10am–11pm
(last ticket 9.30), Wed–Fri
10am–midnight

🚇 Mall of the Emirates

♿ Good

💰 Expensive

HIGHLIGHTS

● The Alpine atmosphere
● The back run is a real test, even for the experienced
● The snowball arena
● The cute penguin march

TIPS

● Ski Dubai is very popular, so book ahead at weekends.
● It provides all equipment except gloves.
● You'll need to show certain skill levels on the slopes—or take lessons.

Snow skiing in the desert—an impossible dream or the height of folly one might think, but not in Dubai. The 25-story-high Ski Dubai indoor ski slope is one of the city's most remarkable attractions.

Indoor marvel Even by looking into Ski Dubai from the viewers' gallery at the Mall of the Emirates (▷ 93), it is apparent exactly what a technological achievement the construction is. Quad chairlifts relay skiers up to the top of the five slopes, including the world's first indoor black run. Runs are up to 85m (278ft) high, 80m (262ft) wide and 400m (1,312ft) long, so there's enough space for 1,500 people at any one time. Everywhere is frosted with snow, created by what is, in simple terms, a giant air-conditioning system. Up to 30 tons of snow is made daily. Insulation keeps Ski Dubai cool even in the summer months—the designers have described it as the world's largest refrigerator.

Fun on the snow If you're not cut out for skiing, there's always the twin bobsleigh track to hurtle down, a purpose-built snowball-throwing gallery, and a 90m (295ft) long quarterpipe for snowboarders.

Snow penguins Ski Dubai also has some rather different permanent residents: a group of Gentoo and King penguins who "march" through the snow daily, every 2 hours from 2pm until 8pm. You can also book penguin encounters to meet these cute guys face-to-face.

Breaker's Bay; families laze and swim in the sun; one of the water-slides at Wild Wadi (clockwise from left)

TOP 25

Wild Wadi

Dubai's first water park, Wild Wadi is a 5ha (12-acre) complex, with rides and experiences for adults and children. This is an excellent day out and a thrilling way to cool down with the family.

Adrenalin rush Key attractions that you might have to wait in line for are the Jumeirah Sceirah (pronounced "scarer") ride, with a 32m (105ft) drop and speeds of 80kph (50mph); the White Water Wadi, which connects to 11 water slides, and the Flood River Flyer, which connects to six slides: strong swimmers only here, please. If you're not scared of the dark, try running the Tunnel of Doom, an underground tube of twists and turns in total darkness. Several rides around the park also contain high-powered water jets to shoot guests along, pushing you uphill or accelerating you through the tubes.

Family fun Visitors can enjoy the family play area in Juha's Dhow and Lagoon, ride Juha's Journey lazy river, or explore the Wadi Wash and Fossil Rock; a "storm" breaks here every hour, with thunder, lightning and even a flash flood. For whitewater rafting experiences, try Flood River.

Making waves The best reason to get wet at Wild Wadi is Breaker's Bay, the largest wave pool in the Middle East, where you can enjoy man-made waves rolling in regularly and relent-lessly. Learn to surf in the specially designed WipeOut and Riptide Flowrider where the constant flow allows you to perfect that technique.

THE BASICS

www.wildwadi.com

🔲 e1

✉ Beach Road

☎ 348 4444

🕐 Nov–Feb daily 10–6; Mar–May and Sep–Oct daily 10–7; Jun–Aug daily 10–8

♿ Few

♿ Good

💲 Expensive

🏨 Jumeirah Beach Hotel

TIPS

● Entrance price is governed by height not age. Anyone under 1.1m (3.6ft) pays a reduced rate; this is because some rides in Wild Wadi have this set as their minimum height.

● There are weight limits on some rides.

More to See

DUBAI MARINA

The centerpiece of a second axis to the city, Dubai Marina combines leisure and residential facilities on a waterway that runs inland around the luxury hotels of Al Sufouh. It's a man-made harbor surrounded by a forest of almost 100 skyscrapers and a 7km (4.3-mile) walkway. On the sea-side, Jumeirah Beach Residence is a complex of five high-rise towers linked by The Walk, a boulevard of shopping and dining opportunities with around 300 outlets. Offshore Bluewaters Island is rising from the ocean. When completed it will be home to the world's biggest Eye Ferris wheel—due sometime in 2016.

➕ a1 ✉ Off Sheikh Zayed Road, west of Al Sufouh ☎ 362 7900 🚇 Damac 🚊 Dubai Tram ♿ Good ⛴ Dubai Ferry Marina Mall

IRANIAN MOSQUE

The most incredible mosque in Dubai, the Imam Hussein Mosque (known as the Iranian Mosque) is also one of the smallest. The diminutive dome, set on a crossroads a couple of blocks from Jumeirah Mosque (▷ 88–89), has a distinctive onion-shaped dome influenced by the Persian architectural style and blanketed in hundreds of thousands of colored tiles.

➕ E3 ✉ Off 2A Street, Jumeirah 1 ☎ 344 2886 🕐 Not open to non-Muslims ♿ None

JUMEIRAH BEACH PARK

This pay-to-enter beach is definitely worth the small fee. The park gets very busy at weekends with locals enjoying the 1km (0.6-mile) sandy beach, playing games in the gardens or cooking at the barbecues. Food and drink is also sold from a number of kiosks. Lifeguards patrol the beach from early morning to sunset; swimming is not permitted after this time.

➕ j1 ✉ Beach Road, Jumeirah 2 ☎ 349 2111 🕐 Sun–Wed 8am–10pm, Thu–Sat 8am–11pm. Sun and Wed ladies only ♿ Good 💵 Inexpensive. Additional fee for sun beds and parasols, inexpensive ⛴ Jumeirah Beach Park

The tiled exterior of the Iranian Mosque

MAJLIS GHORFAT UM AL SHEEF

Dubai's future was finalized at this modest house. It was here, in the late 1950s, that discussions took place about Dubai's future. The complex was constructed in 1955 and was used by the late Sheikh Rashid bin Saeed Al Maktoum as a summer resort when the area was populated by fishermen living in beachside *barastis* (straw huts); today, surrounded by suburban villas, it can seem rather underwhelming.

➕ j1 ✉ Signposted from the corner of Beach Road and 17th Street, by the HSBC bank ☎ 394 6343 ⏰ Sat–Thu 9am–midnight, Fri 3.30–8.30 💷 Inexpensive ♿ Few 🚌 Jumeirah Beach Park

MALL OF THE EMIRATES

www.malloftheemirates.com

Dubai's second major mall (after The Dubai Mall, ▷ 65), with over 550 shops, also puts children on a Magic Planet and slides skiers down an indoor slope at Ski Dubai (▷ 90). The biggest outlets are the department stores Debenhams and Harvey Nichols. On the first floor you'll find the Magic Planet children's zone and the supervised Peekaboo play area for younger children, as well as the Vox cinema complex and Dubai's second theater venue, the Dubai Community Arts Theatre (▷ 96).

➕ e2 ✉ Interchange 4, Sheikh Zayed Road ☎ 409 9000 ⏰ Sun–Wed 10–10, Thu–Sat 10–midnight 🍴 Many restaurants and cafés 🚇 Mall of the Emirates ♿ Good

PALM JUMEIRAH

The first of Dubai's mega offshore land reclamation projects to reach fruition, Palm Jumeirah is the smallest of the three palm islands originally greenlit. The project broke ground in 2001, and in 2007 the first villas were officially handed to their new owners. It's now a fully functioning community, complete with over 20 luxury hotels, including Atlantis, The Palm (▷ 84–85).

➕ b1 ✉ Off Jumeirah Beach Road 🍴 Many restaurants and cafés 🚇 Palm Monorail ♿ Generally good

JUMEIRAH AND DUBAI MARINA MORE TO SEE

Under the Fashion Dome in the Mall of the Emirates

On the beach at Jumeirah

SAFA PARK

The emphasis in Safa Park is on low-tech fun, with bumper cars, trampolines, an obstacle course and a small Ferris wheel. More conventional activities are also possible (volleyball, soccer, basketball and tennis), and you can rent bicycles to get around. Several play areas for children mean the park is very popular with families and weekends can get busy.

➕ j2 ✉ Al Wasl Road ☎ 349 2111 🕐 Daily 8am–11pm 🚇 Business Bay 🦽 Excellent 💵 Inexpensive; activities and bicycle rental extra 🚌 Jumeirah Beach Park

TECOM: INTERNET AND MEDIA CITIES

www.tecom.ae

Two of Dubai's ultra-successful free-zone districts are among several designed and managed by TECOM investments; this whole area is now known locally as "TECOM". These communities have their own infrastructures including hotels, eateries and entertainment venues.

Dubai Internet City is now the Middle East's largest ICT hub. Over 1,400 companies have offices here, including multinationals such as Facebook, Google and LinkedIn. Neighboring Dubai Media City plays host to over 1,500 regional and global media organizations, being the Middle East HQ of giants such as Reuters and CNN.

➕ b1 and b2 ✉ Off Al Sufouh Road 🚇 Dubai Internet City or Nakheel 🚃 Dubai Tram 🦽 Generally good

UMM SUQEIM BEACH

This public beach offers great views of Burj Al Arab (▷ 86) just offshore. It's also known locally as Kite Beach because it's here where the kite-surfers gather when the onshore winds are blowing. Nearby Umm Suqeim Park is a low-key place for families to relax, with a play area and cafés onsite.

➕ g1 ✉ Jumeirah Beach Road ☎ Park: 348 5665 🕐 Park: Sat–Wed 8am–11pm, Thu–Fri 8am–11.30pm (Sun–Wed women and children only) 🦽 Good

Umm Suqeim Beach

Cooling off under the showers

Shopping

JUMEIRAH AND DUBAI MARINA MALLS

Mall of the Emirates (▷ 93) is the flagship of this area, with Souk Madinat (▷ 87) taking the crown for design. There are excellent ranges of shops at Dubai Marina Mall (www.dubaimarina-mall.com) and The Walk (www.thewalkdubai.com), both in Dubai Marina.

D.TALES

www.design-tales.com
Furniture, soft furnishings and home/gift wares produced by Scandinavian designers. It offers a contrast to the multicolored traditional Arabian design.

➕ B2 ✉ Jumeirah Beach Road, Jumeirah (3) ☎ 338 6395 🕐 Sat–Thu 11–8, Fri 2–8

FOLLI FOLLIE

www.follifollie.com
A range of well-finished colorful and coordinated fashion accessories at prices well below the main designers. This is "fashion statement" for the younger generation.

➕ a1 ✉ Dubai Marina Mall ☎ 4324 2644 🕐 Sat–Wed 10–10, Thu–Fri 10am–midnight 🚇 Damac 🚊 Dubai Tram

GOLF HOUSE

Get ready for the greens at this small but well-equipped store. They sell full sets of clubs or accessories and clothing.

➕ e2 ✉ Mall of the Emirates ☎ 341 0611 🕐 Sat–Wed 10am–midnight, Thu–Fri 10am–1am 🚇 Mall of the Emirates

JUMBO ELECTRONICS

www.jumbocorp.com
One of the biggest of Jumbo's many stores in Dubai, this dazzling emporium is filled with home electronics items large and small. And if you've forgotten plugs, leads or rechargers for your electronic equipment, you'll find them all here.

➕ e2 ✉ Mall of the Emirates ☎ 341 0101 🕐 Sat–Wed 10am–midnight, Thu–Fri 10am–1am 🚇 Mall of the Emirates

MARINA MARKET

In the cooler months, Dubai Marina Mall Promenade holds an excellent outdoor arts and handicrafts market every weekend, with local artists offering handcrafted items, fashion accessories and decorative things for the home, and stalls selling coffee beans, honey and other foodstuffs. It's a wonderful place to browse to see what Dubai's creative community is putting out, with the shimmering high-rise towers forming an impressive backdrop. See www.marinamarket.ae.
🕐 Oct–Apr Wed 10–10, Thu–Sat 10am–11pm

MAGRUDY'S

www.magrudy.com
Everybody's favorite bookstore, Magrudy's is where expat kids head for schoolbooks and everyone shops for the latest blockbuster, and it's been this way since 1975. Visitors will love their Dubai coffee table souvenir editions.

➕ E2 ✉ Magrudy Mall, Beach Road, Jumeirah (1) ☎ 344 4193 🕐 Sat–Thu 9am–10pm, Fri 2–10

NATIONAL IRANIAN CARPETS

www.niccarpets.com
Founded in 1917, this family company has established a reputation for supplying excellent handwoven rugs and carpets in the Persian tradition. The family originated in Esfahan just east of Tehran, and now imports silk and wool carpets and rugs from centers of excellence across Iran.

➕ e1 ✉ Souk Madinat, Madinat Jumeirah ☎ 368 6002 🕐 Daily 10am–11.30pm

SNOW PRO

Yes, as the name suggests, it caters to clients of Ski Dubai (▷ 90) and sells a wide range of ski equipment and clothing. Come to the desert to buy your slope gear.

➕ e2 ✉ Mall of the Emirates ☎ 409 4141 🕐 Sat–Wed 10am–midnight, Thu–Fri 10am–1am 🚇 Mall of the Emirates

Entertainment and Nightlife

101
www.oneandonlythepalm.com
There are wonderful views across to Dubai Marina from the deck of this lounge bar. Take the boat transfer from the One&Only Royal Mirage for the most dramatic arrival.
✚ b1 ✉ One&Only The Palm, Palm Jumeirah ☎ 440 1030 ⏰ Daily 11am–1am

2LIV
www.2liv.ae
This state-of-the-art mega club with a roof terrace is the new must-do venue in town. It has attracted great DJ-ing talent.
✚ b1 ✉ Sofitel Dubai The Palm Resort & Spa ☎ 455 5485 ⏰ Tue–Fri 10pm–3am

360°
www.jumeirah.com
A circular restaurant/bar on its own little offshore islet, the upper roof terrace offers unforgettable views of the Burj Al Arab hotel. Guest DJs turn a range of tunes.
✚ e1 ✉ Jumeirah Beach Hotel, Jumeirah Road, Umm Suqeim (3) ☎ 55 500 8518 ⏰ Sun–Wed 5pm–2am, Thu–Sat 5pm–3am

BARASTI BAR
www.barastibeach.com
This perennial favorite is a beach resort by day but one of the coolest beach bars at night.
✚ b1 ✉ Le Meridien Mina Seyahi Beach Resort and Marina, Al Sufouh Road ☎ 399 3333 ⏰ Wed–Sat

11am–1.30am, Thu–Fri 11am–3pm 🚋 Dubai Tram

BASTIEN GONZALEZ PEDI:MANI:CURE
www.bastiengonzalez.com
This celebrity podiatrist's unique approach to foot-care makes it worth the high price tag. The flawless nail finish lasts for months.
✚ Off map at c1 ✉ Atlantis, The Palm, Palm Jumeirah ☎ 426 0000 ⏰ Daily 10–10 🚋 Palm Monorail

CAFÉ CERAMIQUE
www.cafeceramique.ae
A fun concept café. Come for a coffee and find yourself decorating your own ceramics.
✚ B2 ✉ Town Center Mall, Jumeirah Road, Jumeirah (1) ☎ 344 7331 ⏰ Daily 9am–midnight

DUCTAC
www.ductac.org
Dubai Community Theatre & Arts Center is the only nonprofit cross-community center for the arts in the Gulf. It has a changing program of performances.
✚ e2 ✉ Mall of the Emirates ☎ 341 4777 ⏰ Sat–Thu 9am–10pm, Fri 2pm–10pm 🚋 Mall of the Emirates

DUKITE
www.dukite.com
Offering lessons for beginners and improvers, Dukite is the leader in instruction of this incredibly popular sport. They

also rent equipment to experienced kitesurfers.
✚ f1 ✉ Office Fishing Harbour, Umm Suqeim (3), lessons held at Kite Beach ☎ 50 758 6992 ⏰ Daily 10am–9pm

DUSAIL
www.dusail.com
Dusail has boats of every kind for charter. Enjoy an hour trip along the coast or rent for longer.
✚ b1 ✉ Dubai International Marine Club, Mina Seyahi, Al Sufouh Road ☎ 050 551 7280 🚋 Dubai Tram

EMIRATES GOLF CLUB
www.dubaigolf.com
Treading the same greens as the champions is a cinch in Dubai. A new course designed by Sir Nick Faldo now offers more choice.
✚ b2 ✉ Off Sheikh Zayed Road ☎ Reservations: 380 1234

ESPA SPA
www.oneandonlyresorts.com
This minimalist spa offers a variety of facials, massages and body treatments. The hotel also boasts the best *hammam* in Dubai.
✚ b1 ✉ One&Only Royal Mirage, Al Sufouh ☎ 399 9999 ⏰ Daily; women 9.30–2, mixed 3.30–8; last treatment at 7 🚋 Dubai Tram

MADINAT THEATRE
www.madinattheatre.com
A beautifully styled theater with performances

from ballet to Sesame Street musicals.

 e1 ✉ Madinat Jumeirah
☎ 366 6546

NASIMI BEACH

www.atlantisthepalm.com
The spacious terrace overlooks the golden beach at Atlantis. In the afternoon enjoy the resident DJs choice of tracks as you sunbathe. After dark you can dance in the sand.

✚ Off map at c1 ✉ Atlantis, The Palm, Palm Jumeirah
☎ 426 2626 ⊘ Daily
11am–2am 🚇 Palm monorail

PAVILION DIVE CENTER

www.jumeirah.com
The only PADI 5-star dive center in the UAE, where you'll find excellent instruction. The warm waters are perfect for dive training.

✚ e1 ✉ Jumeirah Beach Hotel, Jumeirah Road, Umm Suqeim (3) ☎ 406 8828

SKY AND SEA

www.watersportsdubai.com
You'll find a whole range of water sports at this family-owned company. Take a fun ride on a donut, go sea kayaking or learn to dive.

✚ a1 ✉ Hilton Dubai Jumeirah Resort, Dubai Marina ☎ 399 9005
🚇 Damac 🚊 Dubai Tram

SOCIETE

www.societe.ae
With a range of music from the 1980s to the present day, this venue caters to those who love the retro groove.

✚ Off map at a1 ✉ Marina Byblos Hotel, Dubai Marina
☎ 50 357 1126 ⊘ Tue–Fri 10pm–3am 🚇 Jumeirah Lake Towers 🚊 Dubai Tram

Restaurants

AL FAYROOZ LOUNGE ($$)

www.jumeirah.com
Filled with Persian carpets, and rattan and leather furniture reminiscent of an Agatha Christie film location, this is one of the best places in Dubai for afternoon tea.

✚ e1 ✉ Madinat Jumeirah
☎ 366 6730 ⊘ Breakfast, lunch, afternoon tea and dinner

AL MAHARA ($$$)

The 7-star Burj's signature restaurant serves seafood in a marine environment featuring a central column aquarium. The food is appropriately expensive.

✚ e1 ✉ Burj Al Arab
☎ 301 7600 ⊘ Lunch, dinner

THE BEACH BAR & GRILL ($$)

www.oneandonlyresorts.com
With a wooden deck overlooking the shoreline this is an excellent place for an alfresco lunch or candlelit dinner. The menu is surf and turf.

✚ b1 ✉ One&Only Royal Mirage, Al Sufouh ☎ 399 9999 ⊘ Lunch, dinner
🚊 Dubai Tram

BICE ($$–$$$)

www.hilton.com
Bice is one of the best Italian restaurants in the city. Meat and seafood dominate the menu, although you can still order a simple, if luxurious, pasta dish.

✚ a1 ✉ Hilton Dubai Jumeirah Resort, Dubai Marina
☎ 399 1111 ⊘ Lunch, dinner 🚊 Dubai Tram

BUSSOLA ON THE BEACH ($–$$$)

Sea views and a choice of 32 good value pizzas add to the appeal of this Italian restaurant, which has an open-air veranda. Prices rise dramatically for the a la carte option.

✚ b1 ✉ Westin Mina Seyahi, Al Sufouh Road,

Al Sufouh ☎ 511 7136
🍴 Lunch, dinner. Closed
Jun–Sep 🚊 Dubai Tram

DHOW & ANCHOR ($$)

www.jumeirah.com
Jumeirah's upscale take
on the British gastro-pub
has an urban feel and a
roomy terrace. The menu
includes bangers and
mash, and a daily roast.
✚ e1 ✉ Jumeirah Beach
Hotel, Jumeirah Road, Umm
Suqeim (3) ☎ 406 8999
🍴 Breakfast, lunch, dinner

FUMÉ ($$)

www.fume-eatery.com
Manhattan loft-style decor
and a fusion menu make
this one of the most
popular eateries in the
marina. Arrive early or
you'll need to wait in line.
✚ a1 ✉ Dubai Marina
☎ 421 5669 🍴 Lunch, dinner
🍸 Damac 🚊 Dubai Tram

HANOI CAFÉ ($)

An airy contemporary
eatery serving inexpensive
Vietnamese food. Fragrant
soups and crispy salads
make great light lunches.
The noodle dishes fill a
bigger appetite.
✚ a2 ✉ Gold Crest
Building, Jumeirah Lake Towers
☎ 431 3099 🍴 Lunch, din-
ner 🍸 Jumeirah Lake Towers
🚊 Dubai Tram

INDEGO BY VINEET ($$$)

www.grosvenorhouse-dubai.com
Chef Vineet Bhatia's stellar
Indian restaurant melds
traditional Indian cooking
with contemporary tech-

niques, and it's won him a
Michelin star. Delicate des-
serts help cool the spicy
main dishes.
✚ a1 ✉ Grosvenor House,
Dubai Marina ☎ 399 8888
🍴 Lunch, dinner 🚊 Dubai
Tram

OTTOMAN'S ($$$)

www.grosvenorhouse.dubai.com
The cuisine is upscale
Turkish and Middle
Eastern; musicians playing
traditional Turkish songs
serenade you as you eat.
✚ a1 ✉ Grosvenor House,
Dubai Marina ☎ 399 8888
🍴 Dinner. Closed Sun
🚊 Dubai Tram

LA PARILLA ($$$)

www.jumeirah.com
Steaks cooked with a little
gaucho panache are the
signature of this upscale
Argentinian steakhouse.
The menu has a range
of Latin specialties but
the chargrilled steaks are
the stars.
✚ e1 ✉ Jumeirah Beach
Hotel, Jumeirah Road, Umm
Suqeim (3) ☎ 406 8999
🍴 Dinner

RONDA LOCATELLI ($$$)

www.atlantisthepalm.com
Celebrity chef Giorgio
Locatelli serves up fresh
regional Italian dishes at
the Atlantis mega-resort.
Try Milanese-style osso
bucco or tagliolini with
octopus in a spicy sauce.
✚ Off map at c1 ✉ Atlantis,
The Palm ☎ 426 2626
🍴 Lunch, dinner 🚊 Palm
monorail

SIM SIM ($)

www.simsimdubai.com
A bright, spacious urban-
style café that serves
good-value food from
across the Levant. Choose
from a selection of hot
and cold mezze, or slow-
cooked stews as delicious
main courses.
✚ a1 ✉ The Walk Sadaf 4
☎ 454 2319 🍴 Breakfast,
lunch, dinner 🚊 Dubai Tram

SPLENDIDO ($$$)

www.ritzcarlton.com
With a sun-soaked ter-
race, views over the Gulf
and a menu of simple,
classic dishes, Splendido
has hit a winning formula.
✚ a1 ✉ Ritz-Carlton, Al
Sufouh Road ☎ 399 4000
🍴 Lunch, dinner 🚊 Dubai
Tram

STUDIO ONE ($-$$)

www.hilton.com
A long-time favorite
famed for its well-priced
fast-food menu and its
friendly service, this is a
casual eatery with giant
screens for sports fans.
✚ a1 ✉ Hilton Dubai
Jumeirah Resort, Dubai Marina
☎ 399 1111 🍴 Dinner
🚊 Dubai Tram

TOROTORO ($$-$$$)

www.grosvenorhouse-dubai.com
Richard Sandoval's fusion
ceviche dishes are mouth-
watering, and you can eat
tapas-style, choosing from
a long menu.
✚ a1 ✉ Grosvenor House,
Dubai Marina ☎ 317 6000
🍴 Dinner, Brunch Fri and Sat
🚊 Dubai Tram

Dubai's metropolitan sprawl has plenty to keep urbanites happy but beyond the city limits it's another world. With rolling sand dunes and arid scrubland as far as the eye can see, there's plenty of opportunity for adventure sport and wilderness experiences.

Sights	102–103	Top 25	**TOP 25**
Excursion	104	Arabian Desert ▷ 102	
Shopping	105		
Entertainment and Nightlife	105–106		
Restaurants	106		

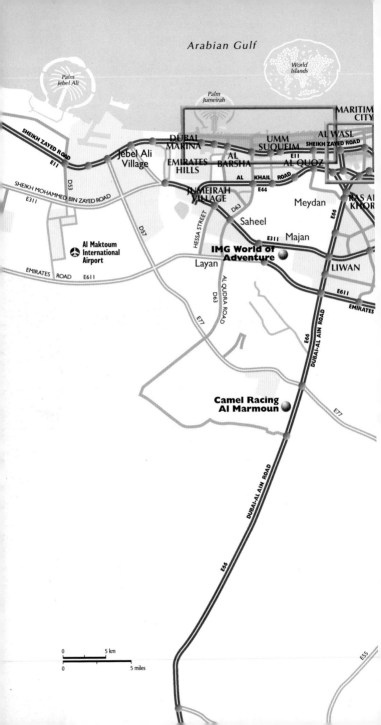

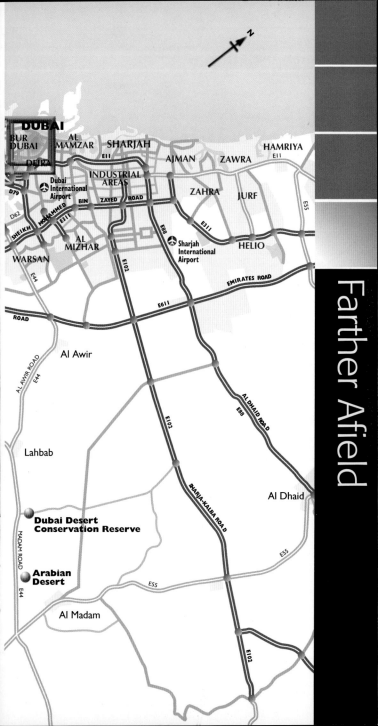

Arabian Desert

You can drive a 4x4 (left) or horse-ride (right) in the Arabian Desert

THE BASICS

➕ Off map
✉ East of the city off the Hatta road
🖐 Activities expensive
(▷ 103, 105)

HIGHLIGHTS

● Seemingly never-ending sand-dunes
● The star-strewn skies after dark
● Relaxing over a mezze meal in a Bedouin camp
● Breaking the crest on a dune buggy

TIPS

● Take precautions in the heat. Think water, hat and sunscreen.
● If you want to see a selection of nocturnal desert animals head to Dubai Aquarium & Underwater Zoo (▷ 64).

It's easy to forget that Dubai is a desert city, but take a short journey inland and you'll discover a completely different world.

Tip of the iceberg The Arabian Desert is vast, stretching 2,300,000 sq km (900,000sq miles) across the Arabian Peninsula. Dubai occupies a transition zone in the northeastern corner, meaning its "desert" is quite varied, with barren rolling dunes sitting cheek by jowl with semi-arid scrubland. The desert supports a complicated ecosystem, though Dubai's largest animal, the Arabian oryx, is critically endangered. Apex predators—desert foxes and two species of cat—are small in stature. They hunt prey including hares, rodents and lizards, though the biggest of these, the desert monitor, might prove too formidable. By day butterflies, dragonflies, locusts and mantises take to the air. As the sun sets, the night shift takes over in the form of several species of bats and desert moths.

Desert activities Today the desert is a playground for Emiratis and visitors alike. Carefully controlled zones have become racetracks for powerful 4x4s where you can put your foot on the accelerator and let off steam, climb the ridge of a sand wave in a dune buggy or glide down it on a sand-board. You can also spend time as a Bedouin at a desert camp with a desert feast, camel rides and falconry displays. It's a great way to forget about urban life even for just a little while. Camps offer lunch, dinner, full day or overnight experiences.

More to See

CAMEL RACING AL MARMOUN

Camel racing has long been a favorite entertainment of Emiratis, and the Al Marmoun camel-racing track is buzzing in the mornings. The camels are driven by remote controlled jockey-machines and reach an amazing speed. Beside the dusty racecourse, the market sells every camel-related accessory imaginable, including attractive multipurpose blankets and saddles.

✚ Off map ✉ Exit 37, Al Ain Road ☎ 832 6526 🕓 Apr–Nov races Fri–Sat 7am and 2pm ♿ Few 🖐 Free

DUBAI DESERT CONSERVATION RESERVE

www.ddcr.org
www.al-maha.com

Dubai Desert Conservation Reserve covers 225sqkm (86 sq miles) of dunes and gravel plains in the southeast of the emirate (4.7 percent of Dubai's land mass) and is dedicated to conserving the biodiversity of the Arabian Desert, including the desert oryx. But it also offers a chance to experience both traditional and modern Arab pursuits: The Al Maha Desert Resort offers camel treks, desert safaris, archery, horse riding, and falcony displays, while local tour companies run trips including dune driving, sand boarding and camping.

✚ Off map ✉ Off Al Ain Road ☎ DDCR: 809 8710; Al Maha Desert Resort & Spa: 832 9900 🕓 Daily, by organized tour ♿ Few 🖐 Expensive

IMG WORLD OF ADVENTURE

www.imgwoa.ae

Rising out of the Arabian Desert and due to be completed in 2016, this will be the world's largest indoor entertainment destination. Based around popular Marvel characters and The Cartoon Network, there will be four zones in all, covering a massive 139,000sqm (1.5 million sq ft). Somewhere to go during the fierce heat of the summer months.

✚ Off map ✉ Off Sheikh Mohammed Bin Zayed Road ☎ 381 1111 🕓 Due to open 2016 ♿ Good 🖐 Expensive (yet to be finalized)

Dubai Desert Conservation Reserve

Camel racing

Excursion

THE BASICS

➕ Off map to southwest
Distance: 90 miles (145km) via the E102; 70 miles (112km) via the E44
Journey time: 1.5 hours by car, 2 hours by bus (E16 from Al Sabkha Bus station to Hatta Terminus—services every hour 6am–10pm)
🍴 Restaurant and café at Hatta Fort Hotel
♿ Few facilities
❓ Stay overnight to make the most of your visit. The Hatta Fort Hotel (tel: 809 9333, www.jaresorthotels.com) can organise guided trips to the pools and surrounding mountains.
The border with Oman runs through the Hajar Mountains, so carry your passport as proof of identity. If you travel by rental vehicle check whether you are insured to travel into Oman. If not, travel to Hatta by the E102 route, which remains totally in Dubai territory.

Hatta Heritage Village
☎ 852 1374
🕐 Sat–Thu 8am–8.30pm, Fri 2.30–8.30
♿ Good
👆 Free

HATTA

The mountain village of Hatta, less than 10km (6 miles) from the Oman border, is Dubai's oldest outpost. It's a popular spot for day-tripping Dubaians.

To reach it, simply follow Route 44 out of Dubai; it's about a 1.5-hour drive. The village is a relatively lush oasis among the dusty, serrated slopes of the Hajar Mountains, thanks in part to a dam in the hills above. There are few attractions in the center, apart from two watchtowers dating from 1880, but on the left of the first traffic circle as you enter the village is the Hatta Fort Hotel, an attractive, 50-suite hotel with restaurants, a golf course and a swimming pool. If you're not staying overnight here—and it is the only place to stay in Hatta—then at least pop in for a chilled drink. The information center in the lobby offers guided tours in four-wheel-drive vehicles or maps and instructions if you're feeling confident enough to drive off-road yourself.

Hatta's main attraction is its position at the trailhead for off-road routes into the mountains. Hatta's rock pools—deep, dark pools surrounded by rocky outcrops—are just a short drive away. On the way you will pass the Hatta Heritage Village, which opened in 2001. This restored mountain village demonstrates how Emiratis survived in the mountains during the last century. A fort, built by Sheikh Maktoum bin Hashr Al Maktoum in 1896 to protect against raiders and invaders, is at its heart. The site itself dates back 2,000 to 3,000 years, but most buildings are no older than 200 years. Traditional building techniques were employed, using mud for the walls and palm fronds (*barasti*) for the roofs.

Shopping

MALLS

Out of town are two main malls. The 275-store, Arabic-themed Ibn Battuta Mall (www.ibnbattutamall.com) at Jebel Ali, on the way to Abu Dhabi, and Dubai Outlet Mall (www.dubaioutletmall.com) with 240 international names offering end-of-season style merchandise.

SUN & SAND SPORTS

www.sunandsandsports.com
Dubai's biggest sports and leisureware company offers names such as

Adidas and Columbia.
🕂 Off map ✉ Ibn Battuta Mall, off Sheikh Zayed Road junction 29, Jebel Ali ☎ 366

9777 🕐 Sun–Wed 10am–10pm, Thu–Sat 10am–midnight 🚇 Ibn Battuta

VIENNOIS JEWELLERY OUTLET

Sells a wide selection of gold-plated jewelry and accessories including genuine but discounted jewelry from Swarovski—worth visiting if you are a collector.
🕂 Off map ✉ Dubai Outlet Mall, Al Ain Road ☎ 56 651 7708 🕐 Sat–Wed 10am–10pm, Thu–Fri 10am–midnight

Entertainment and Nightlife

THE ADDRESS MONTGOMERIE GOLF COURSE

www.themontgomerie.com
Course designed by Colin Montgomerie and Desmond Muirhead. The Academy by Troon Golf offers tuition and training facilities, and the short game areas are floodlit.
🕂 Off map ✉ Off Sheikh Zayed Road 5th interchange towards Emerald Hills ☎ 390 5600 🕐 Daily 6am–9pm

AL SAHRA DESERT RESORT EQUESTRIAN CENTER

www.jaresortshotels.com
A canter among the dunes is a romantic fantasy, but it happens here.

🕂 Off map ✉ Off the Al Ain Road Junction 29 on the Jebel Ali Road (E77) ☎ 427 4055 🕐 Reservations required

ARABIAN ADVENTURES

www.arabian-adventures.com
One of Dubai's longest operating adventure and cultural tour companies has a whole menu of activities including desert safaris, dune driving, desert feasts and falconry experiences. There are booking offices in various hotels around the city.
🕂 Off map ✉ Emirates Holidays Building, Sheikh Zayed Road ☎ 214 4888 🕐 Office hours daily 8–2, activities daily

DUBAI DESERT SAFARI TOURS

www.desertsafaritours.com
This adventure company concentrates on desert experiences and offers a wide range, including a morning tour.
🕂 Off map ✉ Office: Al Murjan Tower, Al Nahda 2 ☎ 50 266 1837

DUBAI AUTODROME/ KARTDROME

www.dubaiautodrome.com
An FIA-accredited track that offers a great range of high-octane rides, from racing Audi R8s to First Drive experiences (ages 12 and up). The kartdrome has indoor and outdoor tracks, with

special sessions for kids (ages 7–12).

🔆 Off map ✉ Dubai Sports City, off Sheikh Mohammed Bin Zayed Road (E311) at Arabian Ranches Interchange ☎ Autodrome: 367 8700; Kartdrome: 367 8744 🕐 Reservations required

THE ELS CLUB
www.elsclubdubai.com
The Ernie Els-designed course ranges over 7,500 yards and has four tee sets. Each hole is designed to emulate an Els favorite on a classic course elsewhere in the world.

🔆 Off map ✉ Dubai Sports City, off Sheikh Mohammed Bin Zayed Road (E311) at Al Khail Road (E44) ☎ 425 1037 🕐 Daily 6–6

JEBEL ALI SHOOTING CLUB
www.jaresortshotels.com
Five ranges with facilities for ball trap (clay pigeon) and skeet shooting. You'll need your passport for identification.

🔆 Off map ✉ Jebel Ali Golf Resort, junction 13 Sheikh Zayed Road ☎ 883 6555 🕐 Nov–May Wed–Mon 1–8.45; Jun–Oct Wed–Mon 4–10.45

SKYDIVE DUBAI
www.skydivedubai.ae
Tandem releases and dives for qualified divers take place on the coast close to Palm Jumeirah, but the training camp is in the desert.

🔆 Palm Jumeirah IFCb2, desert camp off map ✉ Palm Jumeirah at entrance to Al Sufouh Road, desert camp off the Al Ain Rd at Junction 47 ☎ Palm Jumeirah office 377 8888, desert camp 50 154 2992 🕐 Palm Jumeirah Sep–May Mon–Sat 10am–sunset; desert camp Tue–Sun 7am–noon

Restaurants

AL HADHEERAH ARABIC EVENING ($$$)
www.meydanhotels.com
Sit under the stars at this upscale desert camp for a spectacular Bedouin buffet. Price includes live entertainment, falcons, camel caravan and floorshow.

🔆 Off map ✉ Bab al Shams resort, off Sheikh Zayed Road interchange 4, inland on the Umm Suqeim Road ☎ 809 1694 🕐 Dinner (reservations required)

THE BIG EASY BAR & GRILL ($$)
www.elsclubdubai.com
A relaxed eatery overlooking the golf course with a style and menu inspired by Ernie Els' native South Africa. The steaks are excellent.

🔆 Off map ✉ The Els Club ☎ 425 1037 🕐 Dinner, Fri brunch. Closed Sun

DIVAZ ($$)
www.jaresortshotels.com
A wooden dhow floating on Jebel Ali Marina offers an excellent set-price seafood buffet. Eat on the deck or in the air-conditioned interior.

🔆 Off map ✉ Jebel Ali Golf Resort, junction 13 Sheikh Zayed Road ☎ 814 5604 🕐 Dinner

NINETEEN ($$–$$$)
www.theaddress.com
Fine European cuisine at this elegant restaurant away from the city hub-bub. Top quality French oysters are flown in regularly as a signature dish.

🔆 Off map ✉ The Address Montgomerie Dubai Hotel, off Sheikh Zayed Road, 5th interchange towards Emerald Hills ☎ 390 5600 🕐 Dinner, Fri and Sat brunch

Dubai has unashamedly pitched itself as a luxury destination and its hotels are a big part of its appeal. Most hotels have been built since the start of the millennium, and older properties refurbished to hold on to their market share, so amenities are modern and services excellent in all price brackets.

Introduction	**108**
Budget Hotels	**109**
Mid-Range Hotels	**110–111**
Luxury Hotels	**112**

Where to Stay

Introduction

The main question before you book your hotel is… do you want to spend the bulk of your time on the beach and do a little sightseeing, or do you want to spend your time exploring the city or shopping, with beach activities a low priority? You'll get excellent value for money at some of the 5-star and luxury boutique hotels if you choose to stay in the older districts of the city or out in the eastern suburbs. Conversely, you'll always pay a premium if you choose to stay on the coast.

There are more luxury hotels here than just about anywhere else in the world, which means at the top end of the market you'll be spoiled for choice. In the mid-range Dubai has a variety in all areas of the city, from traditional low-rise guesthouses to high-rise towers. In the last decade the options for budget accommodations have improved dramatically. There is a catch, however. These budget hotels are often located in the new business districts rather than in the main tourist areas. It's a good idea to check what transport links are available before you book.

Room prices at the same hotel can vary enormously depending on whether there's a big convention in town or a major holiday. Prices are generally cheaper during the summer when the heat is oppressive, so that's the time to hunt for bargains. You can book all hotels through their own websites—and they'll advertise special rates here too—but it's always worth exploring booking sites for a better price.

TOURISM TAX

The Dubai government levies a tourist tax on room occupancy charged for every night of your stay. This ranges from 7 AED to 20 AED per room per night depending on the standard of your hotel. The tax is not included in the room rate (even when you use a booking site) and will be collected by your hotel, added to your bill at the end of your stay.

PRICES

Expect to pay under 900 AED for a double room in a budget hotel

CITYMAX BUR DUBAI

www.citymaxhotels.com
A modern functional and efficient 3-star hotel close to the historical sites. Rooms are small by Dubai standards, but the hotel has a good range of amenities including several restaurants, 24-hour room service, pool and gym.
🔳 H4 ✉ Kuwait Street and Mankhool Road, Mankhool ☎ 407 8000

EWA HOTEL

www.hmhhotelgroup.com
Overlooking the seafront of Deira (and the developing offshore Palm Deira), the Ewa offers comfortable accommodations at a reasonable price. There's a restaurant and bar and a pool on the roof. It's a 5-minute walk to the Deira attractions.
🔳 P4 ✉ Al Khaleej Road, Al Baraha ☎ 234 3423

IBIS WORLD TRADE CENTER

www.ibis.com
The Ibis is hard to beat for economical accommodations. Rooms are clean, functional and comfortable, though not very spacious. Pleasing touches include Philippe Starck furniture and some stylish bars and restaurants.
🔳 F5 ✉ World Trade Center, Sheikh Zayed Road

☎ 332 4444 🔲 Trade Center

ORIENT GUEST HOUSE

www.orientguesthouse.com
Traditional Arabic guesthouse with beautifully decorated rooms set around a shady courtyard in the heart of the Al Fahidi Historic District. There's a café serving soft drinks and Starbucks coffee. Guests have access to the Arabian Courtyard hotel pool, steam room and gym (▷ 110).
🔳 L4 ✉ Al Fahidi Historic District ☎ 351 9111 🔲 Al Fahidi

TRADERS HOTEL

www.shangri-la.com
Set in a downtown neighborhood north of the creek, this is a well-appointed property with a health club and inside

STAYING IN THE AL FAHIDI DISTRICT

Though they have few of the facilities of modern-built hotels, the traditional guesthouses of the Al Fahidi Historic District are packed with atmosphere—XVA has a more "arty" decor, with Arabian Courtyard being uber-Arabic in design. Bur Dubai and Deira are both bustling districts in the evenings, the souks are especially lively, and everything is easily explored on foot from here.

pool, though it doesn't have the outside space of a resort hotel. There's easy access to the metro.
🔳 N6 ✉ Corner of Abu Baker Al Siddique Road and Salah Al Din Road ☎ 265 9888 🔲 Abu Baker Al Siddique

LAVILLA NAJD

www.lavillahospitality.com
Nestled in the lee of the Mall of the Emirates, LaVilla Najd offers fully equipped apartments along with some hotel facilities such as a restaurant and a fitness center. Perhaps more appropriate for business travelers but also useful for tourists who want to do at least a little self-catering.
🔳 Off map at e2 ✉ Al Barsha 1, Sheikh Zayed Road ☎ 361 9007

XVA HOTEL

www.xvahotel.com
This is the most unusual and stylish place to stay in Dubai. Set in a traditional building in Old Bastakiya (Al Fahidi Historic District), the individually styled rooms are set around three cool courtyards. Rooms are plush and individually designed with numerous examples of art from the neighboring XVA gallery. There's a rooftop terrace on which to watch the sunset and city lights.
🔳 L4 ✉ Al Musalla-Al Fahidi roundabout, Al Fahidi Historic District ☎ 353 5383 🔲 Al Fahidi

Mid-Range Hotels

PRICES

Expect to pay between 900 AED and 1500 AED for a double room in a mid-range hotel

THE ADDRESS MONTGOMERIE DUBAI

www.theaddress.com
Set among the well-groomed greens of the Colin Montgomerie-designed championship golf course (▷ 105), this boutique hotel has sumptuously furnished rooms, an excellent spa and a gourmet restaurant. It's a short ride away from the razzmatazz of the city.
✚ Off map ⊠ Emirates Hills ☎ 390 5600

ARABIAN COURTYARD

www.arabiancourtyard.com
This long-standing Bur Dubai hotel abutting the Al Fahidi Historic District continues to be a popular choice for its location and range of amenities. There's a good-sized spa and pool complex, and the Sherlock Holmes Pub is a busy expat meeting spot.
✚ K3 ⊠ Al Fahidi Street, Bur Dubai ☎ 351 9111 🚇 Al Fahidi

CENTRO BARSHA

www.rotana.com
Simple, compact but trendy rooms make this a good option. It's a 10-minute walk from the Mall of the Emirates and the Metro system. The hotel has a restaurant, a 24-hour deli and bar should you want to eat in. There's also a small gym and rooftop pool.
✚ Off map ⊠ Road 329, Al Barshaa 1 ☎ 704 0000

CROWNE PLAZA SHEIKH ZAYED ROAD

www.crowneplaza.com
Most of the hotels on this stretch of Sheikh Zayed Road are geared toward business travelers, but the Crowne Plaza makes a play for holidaymakers with competitive pricing and a range of down-to-earth bars and restaurants.
✚ D–E5 ⊠ Sheikh Zayed Road ☎ 331 1111 🚇 Emirates Towers

DESERT PALM RETREAT

desertpalm.peraquum.com
Set out in a new district east of Dubai Creek, this well-priced spa retreat

CARLOS OTT

This Uruguayan-born architect came into the international spotlight in 1983 when he won the competition to design the new opera house on the site of the famous Bastille in Paris, France. He's designed several buildings in Dubai in addition to the Hilton Dubai Creek Hotel, including the National Bank of Dubai building and AAM Tower in Dubai Media City.

offers luxurious rooms in a true tropical oasis. With Bang and Olufsen sound systems and iPods in the rooms, they are well equipped too. Amenities include spa, fitness center and riding school.
✚ Off map ⊠ Warsan 2 ☎ 323 888

FOUR POINTS BY SHERATON BUR DUBAI

www.sheraton.com
You can't beat the location of this mid-range small Starwood hotel; Al Fahidi Historic District and BurJuman are within walking distance. With just 125 rooms, the Four Points attracts a mix of business and leisure travelers.
✚ K4 ⊠ Khalid Bin Walid Street ☎ 397 7444 🚇 Al Fahidi

GROSVENOR HOUSE

www.grosvenorhouse-dubai.com
The first hotel to be completed in the burgeoning marina development is a tapering 45-story tower on the waterfront. Facilities are state-of-the-art and Grosvenor House has a particularly strong lineup of restaurants and bars.
✚ a1 ⊠ West Marina Beach, Sheikh Zayed Road ☎ 399 8888 🚋 Dubai Tram

HILTON DUBAI CREEK

www.hilton.com
A modernist's dream, the boutique Hilton Dubai

Creek has architecture by Uruguayan architect Carlos Ott (▷ 110, panel). A riot of glass and steel inside, bedrooms have dramatic black-and-white bathrooms and service is personal and professional. ✚ L6 ✉ Baniyas Road ☎ 227 1111

INTERCONTINENTAL DUBAI FESTIVAL CITY
www.ichotels.com
The Intercontinental rises over the eastern reaches of Dubai Creek, surrounded by the shopping and entertainment of Festival City and close to the Yacht Club and Golf Course. Interior styling is understated by Dubai standards, but still refined and comfortable. ✚ Off map ✉ Dubai Festival City ☎ 701 1111

OASIS BEACH TOWER
www.jaresorts.com
This high-rise tower on Dubai Marina offers large serviced apartments, great for families and groups. It sits above The Walk with its range of shops and eateries. There's a private pool deck on site and guests have access to the private beach of the Jebel Ali Golf Resort, a shuttle bus ride away. ✚ a1 ✉ Dubai Marina ☎ 399 4444 🚊 Dubai Tram

OCEAN VIEW HOTEL
www.jaresorts.com
Set on Dubai Marina's seaside boulevard The Walk, the Ocean View has

over 150 interconnecting rooms, making it very family friendly. There's a kid's club and a kid's pool for younger visitors, and a spa and health club for more mature guests. ✚ a1 ✉ Dubai Marina ☎ 814 5599 🚊 Dubai Tram

PARK HYATT DUBAI
www.hyatt.com
Next to the Dubai Creek Golf Course, this 5-star property is a haven of tranquility within the downtown area. Rooms are relatively minimalist, yet chic. The on-site Amara Spa (▷ 56) and Traiteur restaurant (▷ 58) are renowned. ✚ L8 ✉ Dubai Creek Club St ☎ 602 1234

HOTEL DESIGN

There is no greater concentration of luxury hotels in the world than in Dubai. But the city is also known for a wilful disregard of taste and restraint when it comes to hotel design. Interiors, particularly, can be over-the-top—the interior of the Burj Al Arab (▷ 112) is a prime example. However, chic minimalism isn't entirely unknown here: the Park Hyatt Dubai (▷ above), and the Armani Hotel (▷ 112) are hotels that prove less is more.

RADISSON BLU RESIDENCE DUBAI MARINA
www.radissonblu.com
This high-rise apart-hotel property in Dubai Marina offers superb views and rooms have full-sized glass doors onto the balcony for guests to get the benefit. The contemporary decor is by well-known interior designer Matteo Nunziati. ✚ a2 ✉ Street K, Dubai Marina ☎ 435 5000 🚊 Dubai Tram

TOWERS ROTANA
www.rotana.com
In the heart of the action on Sheikh Zayed Road, Towers offers stylish high-rise accommodations. There are several room types with the Classic (standard) being compact by Dubai standards. Long's Bar Pub is a popular after-work and weekend meeting place. ✚ C5 ✉ Sheikh Zayed Road ☎ 343 8000 🚇 Emirates Towers

VIDA DOWNTOWN
www.vida-hotels.com
An ultra-contemporary six-story Arabian-styled hotel in the shadow of Burj Khalifa. Rooms are cool and neutral, and are well equipped. There are three restaurants onsite, plus a pool and fitness center, and a free shuttle to take you to The Dubai Mall. ✚ A7 ✉ The Old Town, Downtown Dubai ☎ 428 6888

Luxury Hotels

PRICES

Expect to pay over 1500 AED for a double room in a luxury hotel

ARMANI HOTEL

www.armanihotels.com
Burj Khalifa's boutique property is certainly impressive. Styled by fashion designer Georgio Armani, every aspect displays his refined touch. There's an Armani shop onsite, along with eight restaurants and a large spa with outdoor pool.
🞤 B6 ✉ Burj Khalifa, Sheikh Zayed Road ☎ 888 3888 🚇 Dubai Mall

ATLANTIS, THE PALM

www.atlantisthepalm.com
This towering multi-turreted pink property on Palm Jumeirah is Dubai's first mega resort. There's so much to do you might not want to leave, but with over 1,500 rooms, the size might be overwhelming for some.
🞤 Off map at c1 ✉ Crescent Road, The Palm ☎ 426 2000 🚋 Palm monorail

BURJ AL ARAB

www.jumeirah.com
While the exterior styling has graceful lines, the interior is unashamedly lavish. The accommodations is suite only, each across two floors and furnished with extravagant style. All suites come with a personal butler service.
🞤 e1 ✉ Jumeirah ☎ 301 7777

JUMEIRAH BEACH HOTEL

www.jumeirahbeachhotel.com
On the north side of the Burj Al Arab, the wave-shaped Jumeirah Beach Hotel is a vast, luxurious resort, popular with families thanks to its range of sports and leisure amenities and its proximity to the Wild Wadi waterpark (▷ 91).
🞤 e1 ✉ Beach Road ☎ 348 0000

THE OBEROI

www.oberoihotels.com
The Oberoi offers unashamed contemporary luxury furnished in international style. Several excellent restaurants, the trendy Iris lounge, and a large spa with an indoor infinity pool make it an excellent luxury Sheikh-Zayed-Road-area option.
🞤 Off map ✉ Oberoi Center, Business Bay ☎ 444 1444 🚇 Business Bay

WHAT A PARTY

Kerzner Hotels threw the biggest party Dubai has ever seen when Atlantis, The Palm opened in 2008. Said to have cost around $22 million (£15 million), 2,000 guests including Robert de Niro, Sir Richard Branson and Lindsay Lohan watched Kylie Minogue perform on stage, and one million fireworks put the lights of the Marina and Sheikh Zayed Road to shame.

ONE&ONLY ROYAL MIRAGE

www.oneandonlyresorts.com
The exclusive One&Only resort has three different areas of accommodations. Set in 65 acres (26ha) and with a long stretch of beachfront, it feels expansive and exclusive. The KidsOnly activity program makes families with children of all ages very welcome, and the spa treatments are some of the best in the city.
🞤 b1 ✉ Al Sufouh Road ☎ 399 9999 🚋 Dubai Tram

RAFFLES DUBAI

www.raffles.com
The towering glass pyramid of Raffles Dubai is an unforgettable sight, especially at night. Inside, it's beautifully appointed throughout, with five restaurants and bars. There's a PlayZone for kids, an outdoor pool, plus a spa and, most unusually, a rooftop Zen garden.
🞤 H8 ✉ Wafi City Mall, Oud Metha ☎ 723 3537 🚇 Dubai Healthcare City

SHANGRI-LA

www.shangri-la.com
This 41-story celeb-haunt has sumptuous, chic bedrooms. Press a button and your room's curtains will open to reveal one of the best views of Sheikh Zayed Road. The bars and restaurants are popular with expats.
🞤 C5 ✉ Sheikh Zayed Road ☎ 343 8888 🚇 Emirates Towers

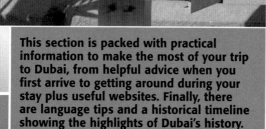

This section is packed with practical information to make the most of your trip to Dubai, from helpful advice when you first arrive to getting around during your stay plus useful websites. Finally, there are language tips and a historical timeline showing the highlights of Dubai's history.

Planning Ahead	114–115
Getting There	116–117
Getting Around	118–119
Essential Facts	120–121
Language	122–123
Timeline	124–125

Need to Know

Planning Ahead

When to Go

The best time to visit Dubai is in the cooler months from October to May. Year-round temperatures are hot, but summers are incredibly hot. There are several major festivals, sporting events and exhibitions throughout the year when hotel rooms are at a premium.

> **TIME**
>
> Dubai is 4 hours ahead of GMT, 9 hours ahead of New York (8 hours during Daylight Savings Time) and 3 hours behind Singapore.

AVERAGE DAILY MAXIMUM TEMPERATURES											
JAN	FEB	MAR	APR	MAY	JUN	JUL	AUG	SEP	OCT	NOV	DEC
66°F	66°F	72°F	77°F	81°F	90°F	95°F	95°F	90°F	86°F	77°F	66°F
19°C	19°C	22°C	25°C	27°C	32°C	35°C	35°C	32°C	30°C	25°C	19°C

April–October The summer is extremely hot and dry; any outdoor activity is discouraged.

November–December Temperatures drop a little and Dubai's outdoor season of sports and café society starts.

January–March Temperatures are the same as November–December but with a chance of short sharp rainstorms, which can result in flooded roads and leaking roofs.

WHAT'S ON

January
Dubai Shopping Festival (can run into Feb): Shops discount stock by up to 80 percent. Events include outdoor music shows and children's activities.

February
Omega Dubai Desert Classic: Usually takes place at the Emirates Golf Club. It has been part of Europe's PGA Tour since 1989.

Dubai Duty Free Tennis Championships: Held at the Dubai Tennis Stadium on Garhoud Road, this ATP tournament features all the top seeds.

Dubai International Jazz Festival: A diverse selection of performers is booked for the three-night festival.

March
Dubai International Boat Show: Your chance to see some of the world's most expensive yachts and cruisers in close-up at the Dubai International Marine Club in Mina Seyahi.

Dubai World Cup: The world's richest horse race, at the Meydan racecourse. The World Cup race itself, always held on a Saturday, is the climax of the Dubai Racing Carnival.

May
Dubai Traditional Dhow Races: The six-race series concludes in June.

June
Dubai Summer Surprises: A reprise of the January shopping festival.

December
Dubai International Film Festival: Inaugurated in 2004, the festival is gaining in popularity every year.

Emirates Airlines Dubai Rugby Sevens: A seven-a-side rugby tournament when Dubai's expats come out to play.

Useful Websites

www.definitelydubai.com
The official website for the Department of Tourism and Commerce Marketing, with comprehensive information for those visiting, living or doing business in Dubai.

www.dubaicalendar.ae
The official "What's on When" website with a full listing of concerts, festivals, sporting events and exhibitions listed by month with connections to official websites.

www.dubaiculture.ae
Dubai Culture and Arts Authority's website has information on Dubai heritage and the wide-ranging cultural scene, including traditional Arabian arts and the contemporary season of exhibitions and performances.

www.guide2dubai.com
Information for visitors and prospective foreign workers, with lots of practical background on customs and lifestyle.

www.uaeinteract.com
A wealth of background information about Dubai and the other countries of the UAE including economic news, politics and government.

www.dubai.com
Easy-to-use information and booking site, with sections on hotels, attractions, and restaurants.

www.thenational.ae
Dubai's oldest English-language press source can still be found in print but has excellent online info, including a "what's on" section covering the coming weekend.

www.dubaiairports.ae
Features arrival and departure information, travel options to and from the airport, and airport facilities including shopping and dining options.

USEFUL TRAVEL SITES

www.fodors.com
A complete travel-planning site. You can research prices and weather, reserve air tickets, cars and rooms, ask questions (and get answers) from fellow travelers, and find links to other sites.

INTERNET ACCESS

All hotels offer Internet access, with most having free WiFi throughout the property. To access WiFi you'll need a mobile device with WiFi facility such as a smartphone, laptop or tablet. The two telecom providers have WiFi hotspots throughout the city at shopping malls and cafés, but they are not free.
Etisalat (www.etisalat.ae) charges 15 AED for one hour or 30 AED for three hours of continuous usage from first connection, or 80 AED for six hours over 30 or 60 days. Du (www.du.ae) charges 10 AED for one hour paid by credit cards, or prepaid access cards with three hours valid for three days for 20 AED, and 10 hours valid for seven days for 50 AED.

Getting There

ENTRY REQUIREMENTS

● Passport holders of the following countries will be issued with a free visit visa on arrival in Dubai: UK (and all member states of the EU), Republic of Ireland, US, Australia, Canada.

● Free visas are valid for 30 days and can be renewed once if you wish to extend your stay (toll free 24 hours EMER tel: 800511 for information about visas).

● Other nationalities should consult the embassy of the UAE in their own countries as visa rules are complex and will require you to pay a fee.

● Passport and visa regulations can change without warning, so always check before you travel.

AIRPORTS

Dubai International Airport (DXB) is on the Deira side of the creek, about 3 miles (5km) from the city center. One of the busiest airports in the world, it's very well equipped. Flights take around 7 hours from Western Europe and 17 hours from New York. A second airport, Dubai World Central - Al Maktoum International Airport (DWC), opened to passengers in 2013, though few carriers fly there at present.

48km (30 miles)
32km (20 miles)
16km (10 miles)

Dubai

Dubai International Airport

Dubai World Central - Al Maktoum International Airport

FROM DUBAI INTERNATIONAL AIRPORT

Transfers to all parts of the city are short with a 10-minute journey by car into Deira and 40–50 minutes to Dubai Marina and the coastal resorts.

DUBAI METRO

● There are Metro stations at Terminal 1 and Terminal 3 for easy access to Deira, Bur Dubai and down along Sheikh Rashid Road (a shuttle bus links Terminal 2 to Terminal 1 for access to the Metro system). If your hotel is close to a Metro station and you don't have too much luggage, it's a quick transfer.

● You'll need to buy a Nol travel pass, 10-journey travel ticket or a day ticket before you enter the Metro system (see Getting Around for more details). There are ticket offices and automatic machines at each terminal. Normal operating hours for the Metro are Sat–Thu 6am–11pm, Fri 2pm–midnight. Trains run every 4 minutes at peak times, and every 7 minutes off peak.

● Metro rules allow two suitcases/bags per traveler and these should be stored in the designated areas. Alcohol is not allowed on the Metro system.

BUS SERVICES
Few bus services stop at the airport and most feed other bus stations for transfer to outlying districts. They are not as useful or as quick as other forms of transport from the airport.

TAXI
Taxis are the most efficient way to get from the airport to your hotel and there are stands outside each terminal and any lines that form usually move quickly even at peak times. Taxis are metered and fares from the airport start at 20 AED for a small taxi, 25 AED for a large taxi, with increments of 1.71 AED per 0.6m (1km) between 6am and 10pm for a small taxi and 1.86 AED per 0.6m (1km) for larger vehicles (fares rise between 10pm and 6am). Sample fares and travel times are as follows:
● Airport to Jumeirah Beach Hotel: 63 AED and 30 minutes
● Airport to Atlantis, The Palm: 87 AED and 40 minutes
● Airport to Bur Dubai: 45 AED and 20 minutes
For further information visit www.dtc.dubai.ae.

CAR RENTAL
Traffic is dense, the road layout is confusing, road conditions variable and driving standards are poor. It's not advisable to rent a car unless you are a confident and experienced driver.

HOTEL TRANSFER
Many hotels have transfer facilities and will have a car waiting for you at the airport. Make enquiries when you book your room.

VACCINATIONS
There are no vaccinations needed for entering Dubai. This information can change so check before you travel.

INSURANCE
Before you travel, make sure you have insurance cover for travel delays and lost/stolen belongings. Check your home policy or bank/credit card policies as these may come as standard. Otherwise buy a stand-alone policy. It's also vital to have insurance to cover medical expenses because, aside from emergency treatment, you'll need to pay for any medical treatment you need and fees are high.

INFORMATION
For airport enquiries:
Dubai
☎ 224 5555
www.dubaiairport.com

Getting Around

TRAM AND MONORAIL

● A tram service (5am–1am) links Damac and Jumeirah Lake Towers metro stations with 11 "stations" (stops) around Dubai Marina.

● A monorail service runs along the spine of Palm Jumeirah.

ABRAS AND WATER TAXIS

● There are water taxi services serving Dubai Creek and the Dubai Marina/Palm Jumeirah areas.

● The traditional wooden *abras* cross between Deira and Bur Dubai on two routes between the north and south shores. Crossings of either five or seven minutes duration. Price per crossing is 1 AED.

● Modern waterbuses operate on Dubai Creek (Sat–Thu 7am–10pm, Fri 10am–midnight) and in Dubai Marina (Sat–Wed 10–10, Thu 10am–midnight, Fri noon–midnight).

● Luxurious water taxis are available (daily 10–10) for transfers between Dubai Creek and Dubai Marina, with 43 stations in all. These must be booked in advance, tel: 800 9090 (toll free).

● All these craft can be hired by the hour for longer private sightseeing cruises.

PUBLIC TRANSPORT

● Dubai has an integrated public transport system with two Metro lines, a network of feeder buses and one tram service linking Metro stations with nearby residential neighborhoods.

● Tickets are valid across the system, with transfers being allowed within the maximum ticket journey times.

● Dubai is divided into seven transport zones and fares are tiered depending on how many zones you travel across, from T0 to T3.

● Journey costs are deducted electronically as you enter and leave the stations or the bus by touching the card against the electronic card readers. For further information visit www.nol.ae.

● There are ticket offices at the airport terminals and main stations and vending machines at bus and Metro stations. Passes can also be topped up online.

● For more information visit www.rta.ae or tel: 800 90 90.

Types of Ticket

● You must buy a prepaid Nol ticket/card.

● The maximum daily cost for all standard travel throughout the system is 14 AED.

● The Nol Silver Card costs 20 AED (with a 14 AED credit to get you started) and can be topped up regularly. It is valid for 5 years.

● The Nol Red Ticket is a paper pass that carries credit for ten journeys of your choice. The pass costs 2 AED plus the cost of the journeys and is valid for the ten trips or a maximum of 90 days.

● A paper day ticket costs 2 AED for the ticket and 14 AED for the travel.

Zone Charges

● Charges are 1.80 AED for T0 ride journeys of less than 1.8 miles (3km), 2.30 AED for a T1 one-zone ride, 4.10 AED for a T2 two-zone ticket and 5.80 AED for a T3 journey that exceeds 2 zones.

● T0 rides are valid for 90 minutes with no connections; T1–T3 are valid for 180 minutes including connections.

DUBAI METRO

● The Dubai Metro has two lines. The Red Line runs from the airport into Deira under Dubai Creek and along Sheik Zayed Road to Jebel Ali. The Green Line links neighborhoods north and east of Deira with neighborhoods south of Dubai Creek in Bur Dubai.

● There are two crossover stations: Union in Deira and BurJuman in Bur Dubai.

● Normal operating hours are Sat–Thu 6am–11pm and Fri 2pm–midnight. Trains run every 4 minutes at peak times and every 7 minutes off peak.

BUSES

● The bus service is designed to link residential and tourist neighborhoods with the Metro system and run regularly on set routes.

● Bus stops are covered and air-conditioned.

● The most useful services for visitors are those that link the resorts on the coast at Jumeirah, Dubai Marina and Jebel Ali to the Red line for quick access to the attractions of Sheikh Zayed Road, and the Deira and Bur Dubai districts.

TAXIS

● Taxis are plentiful (over 7,000 in the city) and cheap, though driver skill levels vary.

● Taxis are metered. Minimum fare is 10 AED around town, 20/25 AED from the airport. Meter starter fare is 3 AED if hailed on the roadside, 6 AED if dispatched. Metered fare is then 1.71 per 0.6m (1km). Fares rise between 10pm and 6am.

● Taxis can also be booked by the morning or the day to make sightseeing easier.

● Taxis will wait outside all hotels, tourist landmarks and malls.

● Pink-topped taxis cater to women and families only.

● For further information visit www.dtc.dubai.ae. The central number for taxi booking 24 hours per day is 0420 80808.

● Rounding up the fare to the nearest 5 AED as a tip for the driver is normal practise.

VISITORS WITH DISABILITIES

With Dubai's modern expansion and many contemporary buildings, visitors with disabilities are well catered for. Facilities in hotels and shopping malls are good and the Dubai Metro is fully accessible. In the older districts of Deira and Bur Dubai there may be issues for wheelchair users with uneven surfaces and high kerbs.

BIG BUS TOURS

The open-top Big Bus tours Dubai on a regular route with informative commentary, allowing you to get a great introduction to the layout of the city, and a hop-on hop-off option for sightseeing at 22 locations. Two ticket options are available for the Day tour, 24- or 48-hour, and these include a dhow tour on the Dubai Creek. The night tour is a 2.5-hour trip and you'll see how beautiful Dubai looks after sunset (www.bigbustours.com).

Essential Facts

TOURIST BOARD

Dubai Department of Tourism and Commerce Marketing operates information offices at the airport (24-hours) and in all the major malls (operating mall hours). The department does have a comprehensive website (www.dubaitourism.ae) and an iPhone app, so you can access information on the move.

Head Office in Dubai

✉ Al Fattan Plaza, Airport Road, Deira ☎ 714 223 0000

Overseas offices are located at

UK and Ireland

✉ 4th Floor Nuffield House, 41–46 Piccadilly, London W1J 0DS ☎ 020 7321 6100

US

✉ 215 Park Avenue South, 10th Floor, New York, NY 1003 ☎ 212/719 5750

ETIQUETTE

Dubai is one of the most liberal countries in the Muslim Middle East but certain aspects of behavior could cause offence, and in some cases result in arrest. It would be respectful not to:

● wear clothing that reveals a lot of bare flesh

● indulge in public displays of affection such as kisses (even hand-holding may be frowned upon)

● get intoxicated

ELECTRICITY

● The electrical current is 220/240 volts and 50 cycles. Plugs are the three-prong type, the same as the UK. Americans will need a transformer to power equipment brought from home.

MEDICAL TREATMENT

● The quality of medical treatment in Dubai is high, with well-qualified English speaking staff.

● Some hotels have a doctor on call and a list of dental clinics.

● Emergency treatment is free but the cost of other treatment is high.

● You will be asked to provide proof you can pay before treatment begins.

● Full health insurance is strongly advised.

● The two main government hospitals are Dubai Hospital tel: 219 5000 in Deira and Rashid Hospital tel: 219 1000 in Oud Metha.

● The private American Hospital (tel: 336 7777) is also in Oud Metha.

● All three hospitals have emergency departments.

● Pharmacies are well stocked and will sell many products without prescription.

MONEY MATTERS

● You can change money at the airport, at banks and at hotels.

● You'll find numerous ATMs throughout the city, in shopping malls and in hotel lobbies.

● Credit cards are widely accepted. Some smaller retailers may levy an extra charge on cards, though they may give you a discount for paying in cash.

● Haggling is expected in souks and markets but malls tend to have fixed prices.

● Traveler's checks cannot be used to pay for goods in Dubai. They can be cashed at banks, exchange centers and hotels but at rates lower than cash.

OPENING HOURS

● Friday is the holy day in the Muslim world so the weekend is typically Fri–Sat, though some businesses close Thu–Fri.

● Shopping malls open daily 10am–10pm, other

shops usually 9am–1pm and 4pm–9pm. All shops close on Friday between 11.30am and 1.30pm for the main prayer gathering of the week.

● Government offices are open Sun–Thu 7.30am–2.30pm.
● Post offices are open Sun–Thu 8am–1pm and 4pm–7pm.
● Commercial businesses open 8am–5pm.
● Banks open Sat–Wed 8am–1pm and Thu 8am–noon.
● Many restaurants serve throughout the day, though some are only open in the evenings.
● During Ramadan many restaurants only open after sunset.

PUBLIC HOLIDAYS

All the major Muslim celebrations change date each year in line with the lunar calendar.

Moveable holidays:
● Eid al Adha (Feast of the Sacrifice at the end of the *haj* pilgrimage to Mecca)
● Ras al-Sana (Islamic New Year)
● Mawlid al-Nabi (the Prophet Mohammed's Birthday)
● Lailat al Mi'Raj (Ascension of the Prophet Mohammed)
● Eid al Fitr (three-day celebration to mark the end of Ramadan)

Fixed date holidays:
● New Year's Day (1 Jan)
● Ascension to the throne of Sheikh Zayed (6 Aug)
● UAE National Day (2 Dec)

SENSIBLE PRECAUTIONS

The crime rate in Dubai is low but take the following precautions.
● Don't carry large amounts of cash.
● Leave valuables in the hotel safe.
● Don't leave valuables unguarded in public places.
● Women travelers have few worries about harassment, but may be subject to unwanted attention if wearing skimpy swimwear on public beaches.

EMBASSIES AND CONSULATES

● UK
✉ Al Seef Road, Bur Dubai
☎ 309 4444 ⏰ Sun–Thu 7.30am–2.30pm
● USA
✉ Corner of Al Seef Road and Sheikh Khalifa bin Zayed Road, Bur Dubai ☎ 309 4000 ⏰ Sun–Thu 8.30am–5pm
● Germany
✉ Jumeirah 1, Street 14A
☎ 349 5050 ⏰ Sun–Thu 9am–12pm
● France
✉ 32nd Floor, Habtoor Business Tower, Dubai Marina
☎ 408 4900 ⏰ Sun–Thu 8.30am–1pm
● Spain
Embassy in Abu Dhabi
✉ 8th Floor, Al Saman Towers, crossroads of Hamdan (No. 5) and Muroor (No. 4)
☎ 2 626 9544 ⏰ Mon–Thu 9am–1pm

EMERGENCY NUMBERS

Police: Emergency number ☎ 999, call center for enquiries ☎ 901

MONEY

The unit of currency in Dubai (and the other emirates of the United Arab Emirates) is the Emirati Dirham (AED or Dh). It is linked to the dollar at an exchange rate of 3.67 AED to 1$. Each Dirham is divided into 100 fils.

Language

The official language in Dubai is Arabic, but English is widely spoken. People are always happy, and proud, to practise their foreign languages, but even if you only speak a few words of Arabic, you will generally meet with an enthusiastic response. The following is a phonetic transliteration from the Arabic script. Words or letters in brackets indicate the different form that is required when addressing, or speaking as, a woman. All road signs and direction markers and all signage at airport terminals and on public transport are in both Arabic and English.

USEFUL WORDS AND PHRASES

yes	*naam*
no	*laa*
please	*min fadlak (min fadlik)*
thank you	*shukran*
you're welcome	*afwan*
hello *(to Muslims)*	*as-salamu alaykum*
response	*wa-alaykum as-salam*
hello *(to Copts)*	*as-salamu lakum*
welcome	*ahlan wa-sahlan*
response	*ahlan bika (ahlan biki)*
goodbye	*ma-asalama*
good morning	*sabaah al-khayr*
response	*sabaah an-nuur*
good evening	*masaa al-khayr*
response	*masaa an-nuur*
how are you?	*kayfa haalak (kayfa haalik)*
fine, thank you	*bikhayr, shukran*
God willing	*In shaa al-laah*
no problem	*laa toojad mushkilah*
sorry	*aasif (aasifa)*
excuse me	*an idhnak (an idhnik)*
my name is…	*ismii…*
do you speak English?	*hal tatakallam al-inglizyah? (hal tatakallamin…)*
I don't understand	*laa afhami*
I understand	*afhami*
I don't speak Arabic	*Arabiclaa atakallam al-arabiyyah*
help!	*tarri!*
thief!	*an-najdah!*
police	*liss*
go away	*ab-eed (ab-eedy)*
leave me alone	*atrukni wahdi (atrukeeni wahdi)*

MONEY

money	*niqood*
where is the bank?	*ayna al-bank?*
dirham	*dirham*
half a pound	*nisf junaih*
small change	*fakkah*
post office	*maktab al-bareed*
mail	*bareed*
check	*sheak*
traveler's check	*sheak siyahi*
credit card	*man*

RESTAURANT

restaurant	*mataami*
I would like	*oreed an aakul*
alcohol/beer	*beerah*
coffee/tea	*qahwah/shaay*
mineral water	*meeyah maadaniah*
milk	*haleeb*
red wine/white wine	*nabeez ahmar/abyadd*
bread	*khoubz*
salt and pepper	*milh wa filfil*
meat	*lahm*
breakfast	*ifttar*
lunch	*ghadaa*
dinner	*aashaa*
table	*maaida*
waiter	*nadil*
menu	*qaaimat at-ttaam*
bill	*fatourah*

TRAVEL

I'm lost	*ana taaih (ana taaiha)*
where is…?	*ayna…?*
airport	*mattar*
boat	*markib*
bus	*baass*
street	*shaari*
taxi rank	*mawqif at-taxi*
train	*qittar*
train station	*mahatat al-qitar*
left/right	*yassar/yameen*
straight on	*ala tuul*
return ticket	*tadhkarah zihaab wa rigooa*
car	*sayarah*
passport	*jawaz as-safar*

Timeline

THE TRUCIAL STATES

Known collectively as The Trucial States, eleven sheikdoms in the Persian Gulf—including Dubai—fell under British influence during the period between the 1820s and the early 1900s. The British plied routes through the area connecting London with its Indian colony (and from there on to British-controlled Singapore, Hong Kong, Australia and New Zealand) and needed the waters to be secure for seaborne commercial traffic, so provided nominal protection to the sheikdoms in return for freedom of the seas.

1820 Britain signs an agreement with tribal leaders along the Gulf Coast. The British Navy protects the coast from pirates in return for a degree of influence in local affairs.

1833 The Al Maktoum branch of the Bani Yas tribal group relocates from farther up the coast to the area surrounding Dubai Creek.

1892 Individual states—including Dubai—sign agreements with Britain to manage their internal affairs while Britain deals with foreign matters. The Maktoum family adopts a progressive trading policy, abolishing commercial taxes.

1912 Sheikh Saeed bin Maktoum Al Maktoum takes control of Dubai.

1950s Oil is discovered in the Gulf.

1952 The seven ruling families of the region, the emirates, form the Trucial Council—the first formal, political bond between the city states.

1958 Sheikh Rashid bin Saeed Al Maktoum becomes Dubai's ruler. Knowing Dubai's oil supplies are limited, his economic strategy is based on attracting more trade and tourism.

1959 Sheikh Rashid orders the construction of Dubai's first airport.

1960 Dubai's creek is dredged at a cost of $850,000. This allows huge cargo ships that can't dock in Abu Dhabi to offload the equipment for the oil industry infrastructure.

1971 The seven emirates gain independence from Britain and form the United Arab Emirates, led by Abu Dhabi's Sheikh Zayed bin Sultan Al Nahyan.

1972 Port Rashid, Dubai's deep-water harbor, opens. Business soon floods into the new port, in part due to the tensions between Iraq and Iran at the far end of the Gulf.

1979 Sheikh Rashid becomes president of the UAE. Dubai's first skyscraper, the Dubai World Trade Center, is opened.

1985 Dubai's new airline, Emirates, is based at Dubai International Airport. Jebel Ali Free Zone is founded, based around Dubai's second deep-water port, Jebel Ali, the world's largest artificial harbor.

1990 Sheikh Rashid dies and is succeeded by his son, Sheikh Maktoum bin Rashid Al Maktoum.

1996 The first Dubai World Cup horse race is run, with the richest prize purse in the world.

1999 The high-tech Burj Al Arab hotel is opened.

2001 Work begins on the vast, man-made offshore island, Palm Jumeirah.

2002 Non-nationals are allowed to own property in Dubai freehold.

2003 Ground is broken on the Dubai Marina and The World projects.

2008 Atlantis, The Palm hotel on Palm Jumeirah hosts a spectacular opening party.

late 2008 The financial crisis rocks Dubai, bringing sudden and dramatic change. New developments are put on hold and existing developments, including The World, are stopped in mid-construction.

2009 Dubai Metro system transports its first passenger.

2010 Burj Khalifa, currently the world's tallest tower, is officially opened.

2013 Sheikh Mohammed announces plans to build a signature Opera House and Art Museum, currently due to open in 2016.

SHEIKH RASHID BIN SAEED AL MAKTOUM

Father of the current sheikh, Rashid (1912–1990) oversaw several high profile civil works that transformed Dubai from a locally important trading town into a regional commercial hub. Though he reigned from 1958, it was after independence in the 1970s that Rashid's vision for Dubai began to bear fruit. The airport came on line, Port Rashid commercial harbor opened on the coast, Dubai Creek was dredged a second time to allow bigger vessels to enter, Al Shindagha road tunnel connected the north and south banks of the creek, and Dubai dry docks welcomed marine building and repair work from around the world. These investments brought commercial success and in turn allowed Dubai to invest in the expansive schemes of the present regime.

Index

A

abras 27, 67, 118
accommodation 17, 86, 107–110
airport 116
Al Ahmadiya School 8, 48
Al Fahidi Fort 28
Al Fahidi Historic District 8, 24
Al Maktoum family 4, 5, 31, 48, 93, 104, 125
Al Mamzar Beach Park 53
Al Marmoun 103
Al Quoz art galleries 70
alcohol 42, 56
animal attractions 16, 64, 85, 90
aquariums 64, 85
Arabian Desert 8, 102, 103
archery 103
art galleries, commercial 11, 12, 36, 70, 72, 74, 75
arts scene 76
Atlantis, The Palm 9, 84–85, 112
ATMs 120

B

banks 121
bars 41
    see also entertainment and nightlife
Bastakiya *see* Al Fahidi Historic District
beaches 53, 92, 94, 97
Bedouin 28, 32–33
bird-watching 68–69
boat charter 96
boat trips and cruises 41
budget travel 44, 109
Bur Dubai 20–44
Bur Dubai Old Souk 9, 25
Burj al Arab 9, 86, 112
Burj Khalifa 9, 62–63
buses 117, 119
    bus tours 119
business hours 121

C

cable car 26
Camel Museum 34
camel racing 103
camel riding 103
camping 102, 103
car rental 117
carpets and rugs 11, 12
censorship 77
children's activities 18, 26, 41, 73, 77, 91, 94
Children's City 26
cinemas 41, 56, 77, 93

climate and seasons 114
Coins Museum 34
comedy club 56
credit cards 120
Creekside Park 9, 26
crime 121
cultural tours 30, 32–33, 89
currency 121

D

Deira 45–58
Deira Islands 53
Deira souks 9, 50–51
dental clinics 120
desert 102, 103
desert safaris 103, 105
dhows
    races 114
    wharves 9, 49
dinner cruises 43
disabilities, visitors with 119
diving 97
Diwan Mosque 34–35
doctors 120
dolphin encounters 26, 85
Downtown Dubai 70
dress code 14
driving 117
    desert driving 103, 105
Dubai Aquarium & Underwater Zoo 9, 64
Dubai Autodrome/Kartdrome 105–106
Dubai Creek 9, 27, 49
Dubai Desert Conservation Reserve 103
Dubai Fountain 9, 66–67
Dubai Mall 9, 65
Dubai Marina 92
Dubai Municipality Museum 54
Dubai Museum 9, 28
Dubai World Trade Center 70–71
dune driving 103, 105

E

eating out 14–15, 17
    brunch 43
    street food 58
    see also restaurants
electricity 120
embassies and consulates 121
emergencies 120, 121
Emirates A380 Experience 76
Emirates Towers 71
entertainment and nightlife 13
    Bur Dubai 41–42
    Deira 56

farther afield 105–106
Jumeirah and Dubai Marina 96–97
North Sheikh Zayed Road and Zabeel 76–78
entry requirements 116
etiquette 120
expats 5

F

falconry 105
farther afield 99–106
festivals and events 13, 114
film festival 114
financial district 71–72
fish market 54

G

gambling 72
Gate Village 71–72
Global Village 105
gold, jewelry and gemstones 10, 12, 75
Gold Souk 50
golf 18, 96, 105, 106, 114
Grand Mosque 35
guesthouses 109

H

handicrafts 11, 12
Hatta 104
Hatta Heritage Village 104
Hatta rock pools 104
helicopter tours 56
Heritage & Diving Village 8, 32–33, 40
Heritage House 9, 52
Heritage House Gallery 35
Hindi Lane 8, 29
history 124–125
Horse Museum 35–36
horse racing 72, 114
horse riding 105
hot-air ballooning 56
hotels 17, 86, 108–110

I

ice skating 41, 56, 65
IMG World of Adventure 103
insurance 117
internet and WiFi 115
Internet City 94
Iranian Mosque 92

J

jet-skiing 53
Jumeirah and Dubai Marina 81–98

Jumeirah Beach Park 92
Jumeirah Mosque 8, 88–89

K
Karama Market 40
karting 105–106
kite-surfing 94, 96

L
language 122–123

M
Madinat Jumeirah 8, 87
Majlis Gallery 36
Majlis Ghorfat Um Al Sheef 93
Mall of the Emirates 93
malls 9, 12, 39, 55, 65, 74, 93,
    95, 105
maps
    Bur Dubai 22–23
    Deira 46–47
    farther afield 100–101
    Jumeirah and Dubai
        Marina 82–83
    North Sheikh Zayed Road
        and Zabeel 60–61
marathon, vertical 71
Media City 94
medical treatment 120
Metro 116–117, 119
Meydan 72
money 120, 121
monorail 118
mosques
    Diwan Mosque 34–35
    Grand Mosque 35
    Iranian Mosque 92
    Jumeirah Mosque 8, 88–89
museums and galleries
    Camel Museum 34
    Coins Museum 34
    Dubai Municipality
        Museum 54
    Dubai Museum 9, 28
    Heritage House 9, 52
    Heritage House Gallery 35
    Horse Museum 35–36
    Naif Museum 54
    Sheikh Saeed al
        Maktoum House 8, 31
    Shindagha and the Heritage
        & Diving Villages 8, 32–33
    Traditional Architecture
        Museum 36

N
Naif Fort 54
Naif Museum 54

national dress 30
nightlife *see* entertainment
    and nightlife
North Sheikh Zayed Road
    and Zabeel 59–80

O
Old Town 72–73
opening hours 14, 120–121

P
paintballing 41
Palm Deira 53
Palm Jumeirah 93
parks
    Al Mamzar Beach Park 53
    Creekside Park 9, 26
    Jumeirah Beach Park 92
    Safa Park 94
    waterparks 42, 84–85, 91
    Zabeel Park 73
passports 116
pearl trade 28, 31, 33
Perfume Souk 50–51
perfumes and incense 10, 12
pharmacies 120
planetarium 26
police 121
population 4
post offices 121
public holidays 121
public transport 118–119

R
Ramadan 13, 121
Ras al Khor Wildlife
    Sanctuary 8, 68–69
restaurants 15, 17
    Bur Dubai 42–44
    Deira 57–58
    farther afield 106
    Jumeirah and Dubai Marina
        97–98
    North Sheikh Zayed Road
        and Zabeel 78–80
    opening hours 121

S
Safa Park 94
safety 121
sand boarding 103
SEGA Republic 73
Sheikh Mohammed Center for
    Cultural Understanding 8, 30
Sheikh Saeed al Maktoum
    House 8, 31
Shindagha 8, 32–33
shisha cafés 13

shooting 106
shopping 10–12, 17
    Bur Dubai 39–40
    Deira 55
    duty free 55
    farther afield 105
    haggling 50, 120
    Jumeirah and Dubai Marina
        95
    North Sheikh Zayed Road
        and Zabeel 74–75
    opening hours 120–121
    shopping festivals 10, 39
    see also malls; souks
Ski Dubai 8, 90
skydiving 56, 106
souks 9, 25, 50–51, 72, 87
spas 13, 41, 56, 76, 96
Spice Souk 51
spices 11

T
taxis 117, 119
TECOM 94
tennis 41, 94, 114
theaters 87, 93, 96–97
time difference 114
top tips 16–18
tourism tax 108
tourist information 115, 120
Traditional Architecture
    Museum 36
trams 118
traveler's checks 120
two-day itinerary 6–7

U
Umm Suqeim Beach 94
United Arab Emirates 4

V
vaccinations 117
visas 116

W
walk: Bur Dubai 38
waterbuses and water taxis 118
waterparks 42, 84–85, 91
websites 115
Wild Wadi 8, 91
wildlife 68–69, 102
    see also animal attractions
wind towers 24
women travelers 121

Z
Zabeel Park 73
zip-lining 84–85

Dubai 25 Best

WRITTEN BY Lindsay Bennett
SERIES EDITOR Clare Ashton
PROJECT EDITOR Rebecca Needes
COVER DESIGN Chie Ushio, Yuko Inagaki
DESIGN WORK Tracey Freestone, Nick Johnston
IMAGE RETOUCHING AND REPRO Ian Little

Published in the United Kingdom by AA Publishing

ISBN 978-1-1018-7938-2

FIRST EDITION

SPECIAL SALES
This book is available for special discounts for bulk purchases for sales promotions or premiums. For more information, email specialmarkets@randomhouse.com.

Color separation by AA Digital Department
Printed and bound by Leo Paper Products, China

10 9 8 7 6 5 4 3 2 1

A05260
Maps in this title produced from mapping data supplied by Global Mapping, Brackley, UK © Global Mapping and data from openstreetmap.org
© OpenStreetMap contributors
Transport map © Communicarta Ltd, UK

The Automobile Association would like to thank the following photographers, companies and picture libraries for their assistance in the preparation of this book.

Abbreviations for the picture credits are as follows – (t) top; (b) bottom; (c) centre; (l) left; (r) right; (AA) AA World Travel Library.

2 AA/C Sawyer; **3** AA/C Sawyer; **4 - 18t** AA/C Sawyer; **5** Urbanmyth / Alamy; **6cl** AA/C Sawyer; **6c** AA/C Sawyer; **6cr** AA/C Sawyer; **6bl** Hannu Liivaar / Alamy; **6bc** AA/C Sawyer; **6br** Level 43 Bar; **7l** AA/C Sawyer; **7c** Viacheslav Khmelnytskyi / Alamy; **7r** AA/C Sawyer; **7bl** AA/C Sawyer; **7bc** AA/C Sawyer; **7br** AA/C Sawyer; **10-11ct** AA/C Sawyer; **10** AA/C Sawyer; **10-11c** AA/C Sawyer; **10-11cb** AA/C Sawyer; **11** AA/C Sawyer; **13t** AA/C Sawyer; **13c** David Pearson / Alamy; **13b** AA/C Sawyer; **14ct** Courtesy of Atlantis The Palm, Dubai; **14cb** AA/C Sawyer; **14b** AA/C Sawyer; **16ct** Courtesy of Atlantis The Palm, Dubai; **16cb** Art Kowalsky / Alamy; **16b** AA/C Sawyer; **17ct** Courtesy of Atlantis The Palm, Dubai; **17c** Courtesy of Atlantis The Palm, Dubai; **17cb** AA/C Sawyer; **17b** AA/C Sawyer; **18ct** epa european pressphoto agency b.v. / Alamy; **18c** imageBROKER / Alamy; **18br** Courtesy of Atlantis The Palm, Dubai; **19t** AA/C Sawyer; **19ct** AA/C Sawyer; **19c** AA/C Sawyer; **19cb** AA/C Sawyer; **19b** AA/C Sawyer; **20/1** AA/C Sawyer; **24l** AA/C Sawyer; **24r** AA/C Sawyer; **25l** AA/C Sawyer; **25c** AA/C Sawyer; **25r** AA/C Sawyer; **26l** age fotostock Spain, S.L. / Alamy; **26c** AA/C Sawyer; **26r** AA/C Sawyer; **27l** AA/C Sawyer; **27c** AA/C Sawyer; **27r** AA/C Sawyer; **28l** AA/C Sawyer; **28c** AA/C Sawyer; **28r** AA/C Sawyer; **29l** Hemis / Alamy; **29c** Megapress / Alamy; **29r** Megapress / Alamy; **30l** Yvette Cardozo / Alamy; **30c** Yvette Cardozo / Alamy; **30r** Tibor Bognar / Alamy; **31l** imageBROKER / Alamy; **31c** AA/C Sawyer; **31r** AA/C Sawyer; **32l** AA/C Sawyer; **32tr** AA/C Sawyer; **32br** AA/C Sawyer; **33** AA/C Sawyer; **34-38t** AA/C Sawyer; **34bl** John Kellerman / Alamy; **34br** John Kellerman / Alamy; **35** Megapress / Alamy; **36bl** PhotoDreams / Alamy; **36br** Tibor Bognar / Alamy; **37** AA/C Sawyer; **39-40t** AA/C Sawyer; **41-42t** AA/C Sawyer; **42c-44t** AA/C Sawyer; **45** AA/C Sawyer; **48l** AA/C Sawyer; **48c** AA/C Sawyer; **48r** AA/C Sawyer; **49l** AA/C Sawyer; **49c** AA/C Sawyer; **49r** AA/C Sawyer; **50l** AA/C Sawyer; **50tr** AA/C Sawyer; **50cr** AA/C Sawyer; **51l** AA/C Sawyer; **51r** AA/C Sawyer; **51cl** AA/C Sawyer; **52l** AA/C Sawyer; **52r** AA/C Sawyer; **53-54t** Art Directors & TRIP / Alamy; **53b** Art Directors & TRIP / Alamy; **54bl** Tibor Bognar / Alamy; **54br** AA/C Sawyer; **55t** AA/C Sawyer; **56** AA/C Sawyer; **57t-58t** AA/C Sawyer; **59** Mathias Beinling / Alamy; **62tl** Yvette Cardozo / Alamy; **62cl** Yvette Cardozo / Alamy; **62cr** Julija / Stockimo / Alamy; **63** Cultura RM / Alamy; **64l** Iain Masterton / Alamy; **64r** Kumar Sriskandan / Alamy; **65l** Urbanmyth / Alamy; **65c** AA/C Sawyer; **65r** Gavin Hellier / Alamy; **66** Nico Alsemgeest / Alamy; **67t** Kumar Sriskandan / Alamy; **67b** Hannu Liivaar / Alamy; **68l** Urbanmyth / Alamy; **68r** Steve Bloom Images / Alamy; **69** Urbanmyth / Alamy; **70-73t** AA/C Sawyer; **70bl** AA/C Sawyer; **70br** AA/C Sawyer; **71bl** AA/C Sawyer; **71br** Iain Masterton / Alamy; **72bl** Iain Masterton / Alamy; **72br** Agencja Fotograficzna Caro / Alamy; **73bl** Kumar Sriskandan / Alamy; **73br** Gallo Images / Alamy; **74-75t** AA/C Sawyer; **76-78t** Level 43 Bar; **78c** AA/C Sawyer; **79-80t** AA/C Sawyer; **81** AA/C Sawyer; **84tl** Courtesy of Atlantis The Palm, Dubai; **84cl** Courtesy of Atlantis The Palm, Dubai; **84r** Courtesy of Atlantis The Palm, Dubai; **85** Courtesy of Atlantis The Palm, Dubai; **86l** AA/C Sawyer; **86r** AA/C Sawyer; **87l** AA/C Sawyer; **87r** AA/C Sawyer; **88l** Keith Erskine / Alamy; **88tr** Robert Harding World Imagery / Alamy; **88cr** AA/C Sawyer; **89t** dinosmichail / Alamy; **89cl** AA/C Sawyer; **89cr** AA/C Sawyer; **90l** AA/C Sawyer; **90c** AA/C Sawyer; **90r** AA/C Sawyer; **90l** Agencja Fotograficzna Caro / Alamy; **90tr** Howard Harrison / Alamy; **90r** David Pearson / Alamy; **92-94t** AA/C Sawyer; **92** Tibor Bognar / Alamy; **93bl** Robert Harding World Imagery / Alamy; **93br** Asia Photopress / Alamy; **94bl** Jon Hicks / Alamy; **94br** AA/C Sawyer; **95** imageBROKER / Alamy; **96t-97t** AA/C Sawyer; **97c** AA/C Sawyer; **98t** AA/C Sawyer; **99** AA/C Sawyer; **102l** AA/C Sawyer; **102r** AA/C Sawyer; **103t** Urbanmyth / Alamy; **103bl** Oscar Elias / Alamy; **103br** Iain Masterton / Alamy; **104t** ARABIA/Balan Madhavan / Alamy; **104bl** Martin Abela / Alamy; **104br** Hemis / Alamy; **105t** AA/C Sawyer; **105c-106t** AA/C Sawyer; **106c** AA/C Sawyer; **107** Robert Harding World Imagery / Alamy; **108t** AA/C Sawyer; **108ct** Robert Harding Picture Library Ltd / Alamy; **108cb** Enigma / Alamy; **108b** Robert Harding Picture Library Ltd / Alamy; **109** Brian Jackson / Alamy; **110t-111t** Westend61 GmbH / Alamy; **112** Gavin Hellier / Alamy; **113** AA/C Sawyer; **114-115** AA/C Sawyer; **116-117** AA/C Sawyer; **118-119** AA/C Sawyer; **120-122** AA/C Sawyer; **124-125** AA/C Sawyer

Every effort has been made to trace the copyright holders, and we apologise in advance for any accidental errors. We would be happy to apply the corrections in the following edition of this publication.

TITLES IN THE SERIES

- Amsterdam
- Barcelona
- Boston
- Budapest
- Chicago
- Dubai
- Dublin
- Edinburgh
- Florence
- Hong Kong
- Istanbul
- Las Vegas
- Lisbon
- London
- Madrid
- Milan
- Montréal
- Munich
- New York City
- Orlando
- Paris
- Rome
- San Francisco
- Seattle
- Shanghai
- Singapore
- Sydney
- Tokyo
- Toronto
- Venice
- Washington, D.C.